AF905828

THE PSYCHOLOGY OF ARISTOTLE, THE PHILOSOPHER

THE PSYCHOLOGY OF ARISTOTLE, THE PHILOSOPHER

A Psychoanalytic Therapist's Perspective

Charalambos S. Ierodiakonou

Routledge
Taylor & Francis Group
LONDON AND NEW YORK

First published 2011 by Karnac Books Ltd.

Published 2018 by Routledge
2 Park Square, Milton Park, Abingdon, Oxon OX14 4RN
711 Third Avenue, New York, NY 10017, USA

Routledge is an imprint of the Taylor & Francis Group, an informa business

British Library Cataloguing in Publication Data

A C.I.P. for this book is available from the British Library

ISBN-13: 9781855758117 (pbk)

Typeset by Vikatan Publishing Solutions (P) Ltd., Chennai, India

CONTENTS

PREFACE

Aristotle has been generally recognized as one of the great philosophers of all times. He is well known as the founder of Logic and for his human approach to Ethics, while his heritage to us is immense with works ranging from politics to theories about poetry and metaphysics, and from biological studies to astronomy and rhetoric. Interestingly enough, although the philosopher wrote the long treatise *On the Soul* and two short ones entitled *On Memory* and *On Dreams* there were no comprehensive studies from a psychological standpoint, however, but only philosophical or general scholastic comments on those subjects.

I first came to know the Aristotelian philosophy some years ago when I read the above works in order to give lectures to psychiatric congresses on the relation between mental health and ancient philosophy. I was impressed by the many similarities of Aristotle's classification of mental functions with that of today's classical psychology and psychiatry, as well as by the philosopher's keen observation of deep intrapsychic processes. So I continued with the study of many more of his treatises (*Nicomachean Ethics; Eudemian Ethics; Rhetoric; Politics; On Sleep; History of Animals*, and so on) and came to the conclusion that, although scattered in the philosophical texts, there were findings, views, and ideas of psychological interest which could be compiled into a body of knowledge with chapters analogous to those found in the textbooks of psychology. The result of collecting such material and commenting on it is presented in this book.

Part I deals with the soul–body problem about which Aristotle accepts a psychosomatic unity (like today's psychobiological model) and in which affects, perception, memory, and other mental processes are in constant interaction with bodily functions. He theorizes Man as an undivided being and that soul and body are interrelated for the sake of Man who should be examined as a whole (a holistic approach).

In Part II mental functions are described in detail according to the definitions in the Aristotelian texts, with a discussion also of the possible similarities and differences with the corresponding mental functions as accepted today. The ancient philosopher distinguishes sense-perception, thought, judgement, volition, psychomotor function, affect, memory, and consciousness as the main psychic processes, but also nutrition and reproduction, which are nowadays considered more biological. Aristotle investigates the interrelation of the various functions; for example, he remarks that sense-perception is basic for the production of images by which memory, thought, imagination, and so forth, are built. One is astonished at Aristotle's ability to observe not only what is evident on the surface, but also to explain intrapsychic phenomena with theories and ideas which are very close to the object of modern dynamic psychology; for example, repression of emotions "in depth", latent and manifest dreams, and free-association of thoughts.

In Part III the views of Aristotle concerning the formation of personality are examined. Material collected from several of his books has been classified according to three axes, which are generally agreed and used by most "schools" of psychology and psychiatry: first, the characteristics with which Nature endows Man; second, the effects of the environment, natural and human; and, third, the more active part undertaken by the Self when the person grows up.

The philosopher accepts different constitutional potentialities for each individual. He brings many paradigms of how Nature influences the personality in indirect ways, while he also mentions examples of persons with characteristics, virtuous and bad, given directly by Nature (for example, intelligence).

The significant influence of the parental environment in the shaping of a child's personality is clearly expressed by Aristotle. He gives advice on how to choose useful games, myths, and tales for small children, and generally he stresses the need for the parents to provide security and emotional support. The philosopher believes that proper education can make an adolescent invulnerable. He makes an extensive description of the curriculum: apart from lessons of general knowledge, he gives emphasis to drawing, gymnastics, and music.

Aristotle is of the opinion that Man goes through a developmental process, during which at various stages his own Self more and more can take over his fortune by undergoing certain intrapsychic procedures (logic against desires, etc.). The philosopher leaves the final outcome to a steering by the conscious Self (rather than unconscious forces), to which he attributes qualities that make a mature man more efficient: freedom of choice and of decision. So for our character we are in some way jointly responsible.

Part IV concerns interpersonal relations. In many of his books, Aristotle considers Man to be a social and political being (*zoon politikon*). This section has been divided into three chapters: Family relations; Friendship; and Erotic love.

A father's love for his children originates, according to Aristotle, from a feeling that they are like a part of himself and so he is trying to raise them, educate them, and make them prosper. A mother's relationship with her children is considered to be the ideal love. Of interest psychodynamically is the note about identification of many parents with their children and about the similarity of personality with consequent affection between brothers when brought up together. Aristotle also registers many aspects of the husband–wife association.

Friendship, a fundamental interpersonal relation, is approached by Aristotle from many angles. He distinguishes many types of friendship and describes very eloquently a great number of personalities, virtuous and non-virtuous, each entering into a different kind of friendly relation and bond.

Aristotle connects erotic love with the passion and drives of youth and describes many emotional manifestations of love affairs.

His approach is what we would today call bio-psycho-social. The biological role of the erotic instinctual drives given by Nature is stressed by the philosopher in a passage in which he considers a sensory function, that of sight, as the one participating energetically for erotic attraction between two persons. The psychological dimension includes erotic feelings that range from passionate love to disappointment and suicide, from care and devotion to grumbling and fighting, or even the killing of one lover by another.

Part V deals with observations and theories of the philosopher which are very close to psychoanalytic ideas and concepts. In a short chapter some such concepts that have been analysed in previous sections are summarized. For instance, the Aristotelian desires and "appetites" fulfil to a great extent the properties of the psychoanalytic instinctual drives. Aristotle describes a struggle between parts of the *psyche* very similar to what today we call an intrapsychic conflict. Free association can be registered in many paradigms given in the ancient text *On Memory*. Many mechanisms of defence are clearly implied in the discussions of various topics. There is a parallel way of thinking on behalf of Aristotle with what psychoanalysis considers latent and manifest dreams.

A comparison is then made between the Aristotelian self-love and the Freudian narcissism. Aristotle is of the opinion that a good and prudent person is in harmony with himself, without inner conflicting ideas, and so he has every right to be a lover-of-self—a notion reminding one of narcissism.

The final chapter is about pleasure. Similarities and differences between the analytic pleasure/unpleasure and the Aristotelian "hedonistic pleasure/psychic pain" are discussed. The founder of psychoanalysis and the ancient philosopher seem to agree on many qualities of that bipolarity. Freud gives more emphasis to the instinctual pressure towards pleasure, but it does not escape the attention of Aristotle that there exists a motivating force behind the whole process. They both speak of pleasure as a rudder or regulator of Man's behaviour.

* * *

The life of Aristotle in its main milestones is known to us. He was born in 384 B.C. in Stagira, a small town of the Chalkidiki peninsula in Macedonia, Greece. He was brought up in an environment of educated people, since his father Nicomachus was a physician in the King's court. At about the age of 17 he went to Athens and entered the Academy of Plato, the best school at that time, in which he stayed for around 20 years. Following the death of Plato he left and worked for some years in Asia Minor and Mytilene making many observations and collecting material for his future writings. In 343 B.C. King Philip of Macedonia invited Aristotle at Pella, the capital, asking him to become the teacher of the successor of the throne Alexander (later known as Alexander the Great). It is most probable that many of Aristotle's views contained in *Politics* and the *Nicomachean* and *Eudemian Ethics* were formed there. In 335 B.C. Aristotle went back to Athens and founded his own philosophical school at the Lyceum (the one called later "Peripatetic"). Most of his books were written during that period until his death in 322 B.C.

Aristotle's ideas and teachings had a great influence on many civilizations through the ages. Not only the ancient Greeks, but also all Latin-speaking people studied his books. The Arabs translated his works and, of course, West European scholars till today find them enriching and continue to comment on them. The student of any Aristotelian text is impressed by its plain and clear style. Nothing is expressed dogmatically and the syllogisms are evidence-based. The ample material which the Stagirite philosopher methodically collected both from Nature and from human relationships is presented in such a systematic way that he has been justly regarded as the founder of the Classification of the Sciences.

Aristotle proves to be a keen observer of human nature. He is objective in his approach and ends up with realistic and down-to-earth conclusions, in contrast to other idealistic philosophers of his era. He has a psychological perspective of people's interrelations, and one is amazed at his ability to register even "deep" intrapsychic dynamics, which are also today the subject of psychological studies.

* * *

The phrases of Aristotle cited in this book have been translated from the ancient texts as found in the generally accepted classical edition of Bekker (1831). The translation is my own, since the language of Aristotle is not incomprehensible for a Greek of today with some knowledge of the ancient grammatical and syntactical rules. Of course, there are helpful translations in modern Greek and in English, but these are usually too scholarly and dry, while the attempt here has been to give the essence of the meaning with the vividness and atmosphere of the subject, as well as paying all due respect to the original.

Notably, wherever Aristotle speaks of *Man*, he means *a person*, that is, male or female, and for reasons of brevity I have used only the male expressions in this work: he, his, him, and so forth.

A phrase in inverted commas has at the end a number indicating the passage from which it was taken, and the reader by looking up the number in the Bibliography can also find the corresponding book by Aristotle. As a rule, text after a colon is an opinion or view of Aristotle in my own words.

Freud's citations are taken from the Standard Edition, as seen in the Bibliography.

I would like to thank all those colleagues, friends, and members of the audience who, whenever I gave a lecture on Aristotle, encouraged me and advised me to continue investigating psychological themes in the corpus Aristotelicum. An advice I am hereby trying to fulfil.

ABOUT THE AUTHOR

Charalambos S. Ierodiakonou is Emeritus Professor of Psychiatry at the Aristotelian University of Thessaloniki. A training and supervising psychoanalytic therapist, he has organized psychoanalytic therapy services in many Hospitals, Clinics, and Mobile Units in Greece. He is an author and lecturer on various topics of psychology and psychoanalysis in relation to philosophy.

PART I

SOUL–BODY

The psychosomatic unity, that is, the quality of the soul-and-body to remain undivided and to continuously interact is a generally accepted view during the last decades in psychological and psychiatric circles. While medical theorization, in order to reach the establishment of such a viewpoint, passed through long phases of exclusively biological approaches and at other times purely psychogenic, Aristotle in various texts of his, written 24 centuries ago, steadily stands on such a position. In his work *On the Soul* he clearly states his belief in a psychosomatic entity and even proceeds to explain (as we will see a little later) why some people have one-sided aspects, that is, some are biologically (as we would today say) minded and others psychodynamically.

CHAPTER ONE

The soul–body problem (*psyche–soma*)

The psychosomatic entity

The philosopher deals with the subject of the relations between the soul and the body by putting from the very beginning a question. He wonders whether all the phenomena of the soul are common with those of the body, or if some of them are peculiar to and carried out solely by the soul. And with humility he answers: "That is necessary for us to understand, but it is not easy" (403a). He then proceeds to the syllogism that since in most cases no manifestation of the soul can happen or act without involvement of the body, for example, in anger, desire, or courage, one may conclude that the soul has no separate existence. To reinforce his conclusion the philosopher brings many more examples of common soul-and-body manifestations, like passion, gentleness, fear, pity, joy, love, and hate. His final statement "because in all those conditions the body is concurrently somehow affected" (403a) is a laconic and clear explanation of the psychosomatic unity in which he believes.

When one studies the text carefully, one will notice that in spite of insisting on the interaction between soul and body, Aristotle does not adopt absolute positions, however. His phrases very often contain words leaving a margin for some other view: "it seems that …"; "in most cases …"; "somehow"; and the like. At one point in the same passage of *On the Soul* he expresses the probability of a mental function acting by itself: "Thinking seems to be par excellence a separate phenomenon" (403a). Yet the philosopher of Logic is immediately ready and open to either support or disprove the above view; so he reminds us of the fact that thought is related to imagination (see relevant chapters later) and, knowing that images are connected with the sensory system of the body, he expresses his doubts about the nature of thought: only if such phenomena were exclusively the work of soul, would it be possible for soul to be considered separate.

There may be an explanation of how Aristotle was led to a probable differentiation of thought from other functions. In his examples of participation of the body, as a rule he refers not to thoughts, but to emotions. He must have noticed (and very rightly so) that in any intense psychic excitement somatic manifestations are present, of the type we today call "neurovegetative". He underlines this point in a passage where he mentions that even after only feeble stimuli one sometimes gets angry and the body enters a state of great tension. He even ends up by constructing a definition containing both the psychological and the somatic parameters: "Anger should be defined as a process of a certain part of the body or its function from a certain cause and for a particular scope" (403a).

The Stagirite must have also observed that, in contrast to somatic manifestations that accompany emotional conditions, during thought processes there is usually no psychic or bodily excitement—a fact which may have made him doubt whether thinking is a combined phenomenon like the rest.

In view of the above, one may reach another hypothesis. The fact that Aristotle in many of his works refers to the heart as a basic organ for mental functions was not accidental or arbitrary. We very well know that the concurrent somatic manifestations he mentions as present during emotional conditions (such as anger, fear, joy, and hatred) are cardiac and vasomotor phenomena obvious to any nearby observer: red or pale face, swollen veins, palpitations with quick breathing, and so on. The Stagirite's accurate noticing of such phenomena may have led to a correct philosophical acceptance of the psychosomatic entity, but at the same time may have been one of the reasons for the wrong view about the role of the heart. These hypotheses are corroborated by a passage in the same text (Book I, *On the Soul*) a little later. There Aristotle keeps his reservations that although emotions such as anger and fear involve in their process the heart ("movement of the heart" [408b] is his expression), thinking "is perhaps either something similar or something different" (that is, without involvement of the heart) (408b).

"Affections are enmattered notions"

The above is a very interesting phrase by Aristotle (403a), which in a few words presents a main position. It is obvious, the philosopher says, that the affections (*pathe*, phenomena, experiences) of the soul are notions (*logoi*, thoughts, intentions) enmattered (*en-uloi*), that is, invested in and manifested through matter. That last word, "enmattered", expresses in the most comprehensive and eloquent way the undivided and inseparable unity of soul-and-body.

In support of his view, Aristotle gives us a series of syllogisms with questions and answers, which remind us of the Socratic dialogues, but in a form of monologue. In this, one can see the persistent difficulty of Man through the ages to avoid the separation of soul and body. The syllogism goes like this: A dialectician and a physicist would define an affection, for example, anger, in different ways. The former would say that anger is a desire for revenge, while the latter would define it as a boiling of the blood around the heart. So one gives importance to the reason and the intention (immaterial things), and the other only to matter. The opposing views of the two, the dialectician on the one hand (who theorizes through a dialogue) and the physicist on the other (who examines the material aspect of even living things, the biologist of today), refer us, with the appropriate example of anger, to similar positions held for centuries after Aristotle's era. In the same way, at the beginning of the 20th century there would be a great antithesis between a psychodynamically oriented scientist interpreting anger and revenge as a discharge of instinctual and repressed tendencies, and a biologically oriented scientist who would not, of course, speak about the boiling of the blood but would explain things in terms of neurotransmitters and the like.

The Stagirite proceeds also to a more practical example from everyday life in order to demonstrate the two opposing viewpoints.

Speaking about a house, he says that the dialectician would consider it a shelter against destruction from the wind, the rain, or the heat, while the physicist would describe it simply as a sum of stones, bricks, and timber. So, again, one underlines the reason and the goal, while the other looks at the material side only. The important contribution by Aristotle is contained in a third aspect that he offers with the example of the house: There is another possibility, he says, for one to consider both the matter and form as well as the ultimate purpose. His own opinion is obvious and in favour of the last proposition of his discussion when he answers in an interrogative way: "Is he not a genuine scientist rather the one who combines both viewpoints?" (403b). And at the end of the chapter he sums up: "Let me repeat that the affections of the soul are inseparable from the matter in animals" (403b).

The holistic approach

Aristotle establishes another approach when he examines the phenomena of the soul, one which modern psychiatry calls "holistic". He argues that we should not say that the soul learns or thinks or feels, but that Man performs all those functions through the soul. Therefore, for the philosopher, Man is a whole and the significant object of examination; soul and body belong to Man, and their processes are interrelated for his sake. This interrelation is evident in the statement of Aristotle that sometimes the processes begin from the body, for example, the sensory system, and reach the soul (producing thoughts and feelings), and at other times the soul initiates a process, for example, a visual representation in memory recollection.

The Stagirite clarifies even more the intercommunication between psyche and soma in two other passages of *On the Soul*, commenting that previous philosophers adapted the soul into a body ("put in harmony" [414a] is the Greek terminology) without defining the kind of the body, or its condition, the reason, the circumstances, and so on. Aristotle, on the contrary, believes that it is not possible just by chance for a soul to be embodied ("to be clothed" [407b] is the expression in the text) in any body, but that the latter should have a specific and fitting form. He recognizes, nevertheless, that in spite of the Pythagoreans neglecting that part of the subject, they had also tried to examine the nature of the soul, and he agrees with them in a basically holistic position: The soul cannot exist without a body, while it cannot be a body; so it is not a body but something relative to a body (414a). He then adds his own view that the soul exists in a body, but each time a body of a certain type, with definite properties and roles.

In his detailed discussion of the subject, Aristotle comes up with a laconic, yet very clear, exposition of his concept about the interrelation of soul-and-body, attributing to soul energetic initiative: the soul acts and the body is acted upon; the former activates a process and the latter is performing the process. He even further stresses the fact that soul and body do not communicate with each other by chance, but rather in a deliberate way. For that he makes a comparison with carpentry: each art must use its own tools and each soul its own body.

The "composition" of soul and body

Apart from the functional aspect of the relation between soul and body, Aristotle wants to investigate their "composition"—whether they are parts of the same substance. He puts forward an existential question, probably being affected by the phenomena of old age and death: How is it that when the one perishes the other disappears, and when the soul is no more in action the body dissolves? Such problems have such (and so difficult) perplexities, the philosopher admits. He, nevertheless, continues to examine the subject through a series of syllogisms in an exemplary way, even though there can be no answers to all.

At the end Aristotle rejects the view that the soul is composed of parts of the body, and considers it absurd to accept that mental functions—like thought, sense-perception, and desire—can be a mixture of inorganic elements with just a different ratio than, say, flesh or bones. But the philosopher continues to wonder: "If the soul is not a mixture of elements at a certain ratio, how is it (and what is it) that something perishes as soon as the soul departs from man?" (408a) The answer is given a little later in the text following new syllogisms with examples which lead to interesting conclusions, especially regarding thought. The argument is that thought must be a kind of innate substance, non-perishable, because otherwise it would be destroyed by old age, as for instance happens with vision. The Stagirite contends that the soul is not affected in old age and that the inabilities of old people are due to suffering "of that in which the soul is contained, like it happens in illnesses" (408b). So when one can no more contemplate, remember, love, or hate, the cause is not an affection of the soul but of the body. Those functions are not dependent only on one part (soul or body), but to *a composite state* which has been lost. And the philosopher concludes in a kind of literary phrase: "So the intellect perhaps is something more divine and is invulnerable" (408b)!

This last excellent expression by Aristotle attributes to the intellectual functions qualities of a very high level, above any material aspect of the human being. Considering that such a phrase comes from a thinker without theocratic beliefs, his admiration for the human mind originates in his respect for the gifts of Nature, which (as we will later see) he examined diligently all through his life. Maybe that is why he uses the adjective in the comparative "*more* divine"—and not simply in the positive—"divine".

The essential conclusion of the whole syllogism lies in the phrase explaining that the mental activities do not belong to one constituent part but to a composite condition (*tou koinou*) of soul-and-body, a view which is in total agreement with the psychosomatic approach of today. It is worth mentioning that Aristotle in that passage of the text of Book I (*On the Soul*) does not use the word "soma", but instead says "that which has/contains the soul" (408b). Some commentators, for that reason, speak not of "body" but rather of "subject", "person", "vehicle", and so on. I think that we should not hesitate to use the word "body", since the comparison the philosopher makes (with that which can suffer an illness, meaning of course the body) is very elucidating. The advantage of not naming the body by Aristotle with a specific term facilitates even further, I believe, the acceptance of the human being as an undivided entity. (Personally, I find it difficult whenever, although speaking about an "entity", I have to use "psychosomatic" or "soul-and-body", both of which inevitably convey an idea of two parts.)

Another interesting aspect of the philosopher's approach to the subject is a small phrase of three words: "in whatever way (the soul is contained in the body)" (408b); it shows how honest and cautious he is in admitting his ignorance of further processes, for such a complex problem cannot be easily solved and one cannot be dogmatic about it.

In Book II of the same work Aristotle is more specific and uses the phrase "physical bodies". He elaborates on the functional unity of soul and body and their common activities, attributing the initiating role to the soul. The physical bodies, he says, are instruments of the soul (both in animals and plants) and they exist *for the sake of the soul*, a comment which should be taken in two ways—*for the benefit* of the soul and *because* of the soul. So the philosopher becomes more analytic in this passage and expresses something analogous to the position discussed previously (the soul acts—the body is acted upon): that the soul is the cause for the existence and the activating agent of the organs of the body, and that they all function for the soul's sake, which is the ultimate purpose of Nature.

PART II

MENTAL FUNCTIONS

Psychology and psychiatry deal with the manifestations of the *psyche* and, therefore, examine the mental functions of human beings, normal and abnormal, and classify them into certain categories. In spite of the differences of various so-called "schools" of psychology, the mental functions have, for decades, been distinguished in approximately the same way, especially for the purposes of the "present state" examination of an individual: thought, volition, affect, sense-perception, judgement, and so forth.

In this section of the book, I will try to discuss the mental functions as described, directly or indirectly, in Aristotle's work *On the Soul*, by studying the content of each one and locating the possible similarities or differences with the corresponding mental functions as accepted today. Unfortunately, the description and analysis of these functions is done in a scattered way by the philosopher in his text, but his intention to classify them is clear enough: "the parts of the *psyche* ... when we are going to divide and separate them according to functions" (433b) and, in another passage, "the functions of the soul ... as we have said: sense-perception, desire, thought ..." (414a).

Dynameis is the term Aristotle uses for mental functions, a term usually also translated as "faculties" or "potentialities". ("Potentialities" is the literally most correct, since *dynamei* in ancient but also modern Greek means "potentially".) The number of the soul's functions is a great one according to the philosopher, and not just two—logical and non-logical—as some philosophers insisted, or three—logic, affects, and desires—as many (probably including Plato) claimed.

From the total text of *On the Soul* one can gather quite a few mental functions, which, in a very interesting way, correspond to those that modern mental health professionals consider basic. I describe in the following pages eight functions, as well as an additional two, which, although Aristotle enumerates among the rest of the *dynameis*, today are considered more biological than purely mental.

CHAPTER TWO

Sense-perception

Aristotle gives great importance to the function of sense-perception; he considers it as the primary basis for other functions, like imagination, memory, and thought. For that reason he devotes a rather long treatise to *Sense and Sensibilia* (*Peri aestheseos kai aestheton*); but also in his work *On the Soul* many chapters (in Books II and III) deal with subjects of special interest to psychology.

The philosopher starts the discussion by stating that sense-perception is the result of an activation and a process which leads to change (*alloiosis*) in the organism, functional and possibly structural—as one can gather from his whole exposition. Sense-perception is considered an active phenomenon and not one passively produced by an external stimulus, as other philosophers of his time thought. That is why, according to Aristotle, both the function of sense-perception and the perceptible object must be viewed at a certain moment as being "in a potential state" (*dynamei* [417a]) and at other times as "in action" (*energeia* [417a]). So a sensory organ does not function by itself, but is always alert and ready to accept a stimulus and be activated for a percept to be produced. When stimulation starts, both the stimulating object and the sensory organ are in action until the process is completed and the external object has become perceptible by the person.

Aristotle describes five senses, the same way that modern physiology does: sight, hearing, smell, taste, and touch. We are able to perceive objects through the sensory organs either by directly touching them, as in the case of the sense of touch, or by various intermediate elements in the case of the other senses. Air and water are mentioned as such natural elements, because they are transparent (especially for sight and hearing), and to a less extent earth and fire.

The perceptible objects

Three categories of perceptible objects can be distinguished according to Aristotle:

1. those which are "particular" to each sense and which can only be perceived by that sense (for example, a visible object by sight, or a tangible one by touch)
2. the "commonly perceived", that is, those that can be perceived by more than one sense
3. those perceived "by chance", depending on the circumstances, some coincidences, and so on.

In the first category, perceptibles can be perceived by only one sense, for example, colour only by sight, and sounds only by hearing. In this way, the philosopher rightly comments, there is no possibility for a sense to be deceived or misled as to, for example, whether an object is blue or is red, or what sound it produces. Regarding the sense of touch, Aristotle proceeds to a differentiation by bringing in examples in his text that this sense is able to perceive many and opposite conditions, such as hot–cold, dry–wet, and soft–hard. (The philosopher could not, of course, explain at that time his very correct observation in terms of physiology and anatomy, as we can today—knowing the various kinds of sensory nerve-ends in the skin.)

The Stagirite does not take anything for granted, unless he has previously searched the "hows, whys, when". So in this instance he asks himself: "Why do we have many senses and not only one?" (425b) And he answers his question, although in an interrogative way—always preferring not to be dogmatic: "Perhaps, so that we make less mistakes regarding what follows" (425b). To make things clearer he gives the following example: Whatever is yellow could be taken (by sight alone) to be some bile, but we will be deceived if we do not taste it.

The second category consists of the "commonly perceived" and Aristotle enumerates as such the movement of objects, their shape, size, and number. These are qualities of objects for which no certain or specialized sense is needed in order for them to be perceived; a common ability exists in many senses to spot such qualities. For instance, movement can be understood by seeing an object, but also by touching it—even with the eyes closed, or by hearing (or not hearing) a sound of movement, and so on.

The third category of perceptibles "by chance" concerns objects that one relates with certain of their qualities, which had in the past been accidentally perceived by two or more sensory organs at the same time, that is, coincidentally and often by chance. The following example is in the text: We may be able to perceive that something is sweet by simply seeing it at the present time if, in the past, two at least senses acted coincidentally, that is, if we had before seen and tasted that object.

Aristotle, nevertheless, warns us that perceptibles do not always have credibility and validity, especially those of the first category. In order to illustrate that he mentions the case of the son of somebody called Cleon, who had a white complexion, and whom one might say one recognized from far away because of his whiteness. The Stagirite stresses the fact that in such cases, when only one sense is involved (seeing somebody being white, in the example), it may most probably lead to a mistake and that we need two simultaneously acting senses in order to be sure. He underlines that when they coincide, then we are in a better position to recognize.

On the occasion of this discussion, the ancient philosopher in addition remarks that simultaneous action of more than one sensory organ is necessary, "since there is no other sense to tell us that both qualities belong to one and the same object" (425b). With this phrase, I believe, Aristotle, with his acuity, wonders for a moment and is expressing the need for a co-ordinating organ of the senses—even by stressing its absence. Yet the way he puts the subject shows that he was searching for a co-ordinating organ among the sensory system, obviously ignoring the co-ordinating role of the brain that we today know.

Relation to other functions

Aristotle, a keen observer of human phenomena, classifies them in a remarkably complete way and examines their relations with each other. Sense-perception is such a paradigm; in many passages of his work *On the Soul* he relates sense-perception with the function of thought and of judgement. He says, for instance, that something sweet will activate both sense-perception and thought, adding in that chapter that one judges according to what one perceives and thinks. We accept today something very similar: that the ability to distinguish percepts may start from the senses but it ends up as a thinking, conceptual process. In the treatise *On Memory* Aristotle describes how sense-perception is basic for the production of images in the mind, that is, mental representations which are retained and later recalled, so that memory can be effected. On the other hand, in his discussion *On Dreams* the Greek philosopher underlines the affect of emotions on sense-perception; he brings examples of how the senses are easily deceived when one is in great passion, in fear, in love, or in anger.

Aristotle raises an interesting philosophical question which he answers in a (what we would today call) neurophysiological way. He cites the beliefs of physical philosophers before him, who taught that an object does not exist at a certain moment if no-one is perceiving it at that time. With due respect to older teachers, he comments that what they said is both right and not right (426a). And he gives the following explanation: We must face the subject in a double way. It may really happen what earlier philosophers said and a person may not be seeing an object, but that object continues to exist in a potential state, ready to be actively seen as soon as the sight of the person begins to function. He further elucidates the notions he introduces ("potential" and "active state" [417a]) with the following example: A person who potentially has the faculty of hearing may not be listening at a certain moment, and an object which can make a sound does not sound all the time, but when the person potentially able to listen gets in action, and also does the object, then one can say that what actively happens is simultaneous hearing and sounding.

Imagination

Imagination is not accepted by many schools of psychology today as a separate faculty, and in most psychiatric case reports no mention is made of imagination as an entity by itself. It seems that Aristotle also had his doubts on this issue, although he enumerates imagination at the same level along with the rest of the functions (*dynameis*, "potentialities"). At one point in the work *On the Soul*, he says that the subject is "unclear" and that there is a need for further discussion, but he also declares that, irrespective of classification, the fact is that there can be no imagination without involvement of the senses. A more detailed exposition can be found in another passage in which the philosopher underlines the relation of imagination to other functions. Repeating that imagination cannot exist without previous sense-perceptive processes, he goes on stressing the fact that the faculties of thought and, furthermore, volition, are to some extent depending on those two in order to function.

A step-by-step description of the process of imagination is given in the treatises *On Memory* and *On Dreams*: Following stimulation by an external stimulus a sensory organ is activated and a corresponding process starts having, as a result, the production of a percept. The latter (seeing, hearing, etc.) lasts as long as the stimulus is in action, but this type of direct perceiving stops as soon as the stimulus is no more affecting. Nevertheless, there remains in the mind a mental representation of the percept (visual, auditory, etc.) which the Stagirite calls *phantasma*, an image; so the process of perceiving may continue by the function of imagination (*phantasia*), which uses images in an immaterial way (not biological). The ancient philosopher in conclusion states that, epigrammatically: "Images are like percepts but without a material basis" (432a). Most images that we hold in mind are visual, and they are "as if we are seeing in pictures (or in written words) the terrible or the encouraging things" (427b). (See Chapter Six for a further discussion about images.)

In view of the above, Aristotle defines the content of imagination as the total of images that resulted from stimulation of the sensory system. He points to the usefulness of this content by saying that a person having at his disposal the images as a continuation of the percepts "has the possibility of doing or suffering a lot" (428b). We accept today that images are involved in memory regarding past events, as well as in thought and volition regarding decisions for actions in the future. The ancient philosopher relates imagination with those faculties in the same temporal way. For memory, as we will see in Chapter Six, he accepts that images are basic in its formation. Images are imprinted and retained in the mind until they are recalled. (At one point, he considers both imagination and memory as being in the same area of the soul.)

Regarding the faculty of thought, Aristotle notes that its capacity to understand depends on images and that these determine, in the absence of any active sense, what a thinking person will decide about the future—whether to pursue or avoid something. The philosopher brings the example of somebody who upon seeing a torch burning and moving understands that an enemy is approaching, based on images kept from the past that help him in his next move. The Stagirite further elaborates on the connection of imagination and thought by insisting that, although images resembling the percepts remain in the mind, logical thinking must take place in order for the right decisions to be taken. That, he continues, does not happen in the case of wild animals, which do not possess logical thought and are guided largely by images. The same, he adds, is seen in men when sometimes their logic is covered by disease or passion.

CHAPTER THREE

Thought and judgement

The faculty of thought together with those of affects and volition occupy the main interest of psychologists and psychiatrists, especially when they examine the present mental state of a patient. Modern psychiatry distinguishes two basic parameters of thought: i) coherence, which concerns the stream of talk and the way that thoughts are connected to each other, and ii) content of thought, which may be normal, logical, and corresponding to reality, or abnormal with delusions, phobias, obsessive ideas, and so on. Aristotle, of course, as a philosopher, has a different starting point, but still the various issues he raises about thought are of great interest to anyone who more deeply studies the mental functions: the nature of thought, its attributes, its various types (understanding, knowledge, etc.), the relation of thought to other faculties, the somatic involvement (or not) in thinking, and so forth. A great part of the work *On the Soul* (in Book III 3–7, 10) is devoted to such questions, but they are scattered in the text and here an attempt is being made to collect in a sequence what is psychologically important, with due respect to the prototype.

Aristotle gives the following definition: "I call thought that by which the soul (mind) thinks and conceives" (429a). And in another passage he considers the function of thought as "that part of the soul by which it knows and understands (prudently)" (429a).

A significant and elucidating position of the philosopher can be found in the comparison he makes between thought and sense-perception, in which he opposes the view of earlier philosophers who identified the two as one and the same. He says of the earlier philosophers: "Thought is regarded as a form of perceiving, because by both the soul can discriminate things and know them better" (427a). He mentions Empedocles and Homer as having that belief and explains that the reason for their wrong view was their looking upon thinking as a somatic process, like perceiving.

The Stagirite's argument against a bodily existence of thought (about which we will later discuss in detail) goes like this: It is obvious that perceiving and understanding are not identical, since the former is to be found in all animals, while the latter is to be found in only a small number. In a similar way thinking—which may be right or wrong—is not the same as perceiving; perception of the "particular" objects proves always to be true and exists in all animals, while thought may sometimes be false and can be found only in creatures with reason.

There are three types by which the faculty of thought (*nous, noein*) presents itself according to Aristotle: knowledge, opinion, and understanding. I use here the terms as given in the Oxford translation of *On the Soul* for the Greek: *episteme, doxa,* and *phronesis* correspondingly. There are very often problems in translating from ancient Greek and the exact meaning cannot always be captured on translation. Also all scholars admit that (for various reasons, which they try to explain) in the Corpus Aristotelicum one may find a Greek term being used with different contents in pages of the same book. For instance, the term *nous* frequently is met meaning "thought" and at other places "mind". Again, *nous* is interchanged with *phronein* and *dokein* without any obvious explanation.

Regarding the three types of *noein* (thinking), I will try below to examine their meaning, as close as possible to what the Stagirite really wanted to impart, by selecting several passages from his books. It should be noted that in the text *episteme, doxa,* and *phronesis* are characterized by the author as "right thinking" (427b), while, on the contrary, "the opposites are not correct" (427b), and, as such, ignorance, wrong opinion, and wrong (or imprudent) understanding are meant.

Knowledge—episteme

The Greek word *episteme* (from the verb *epistamai*) literally means "to stand above", therefore, to be at height and able to see widely and deeply, that is, to know things thoroughly. Knowledge, I believe, was rightly adopted as translating *episteme* for the total sum of thoughts, well established and evidence-based (as we would today scientifically say), which one possesses. (It is not accidental that in modern Greek *episteme* is the only word used to denote science.)

The content of the term in the Aristotelian writings concerns persons who are educated, of high intelligence, and have the ability and will to face various subjects, contemplating them deeply and covering their whole spectrum. An interesting description of the personality characteristics of such persons can be found in Book II of *On the Soul*. Aristotle first considers that man is par excellence a being able to possess knowledge. One type of personality is at any time actively reflecting and contemplating, so he is in the most proper sense *epistemon* ("knower", "scientist"). Two other types of personality are only potentially capable of thinking deeply and theorizing. One person, because of what he has inherited and what Nature has bestowed, shall theorize on the condition that he changes considerably his bad habits and accepts lessons and instructions. The other, having knowledge of arithmetic and grammar and potentially able to theorize (if, of course, nothing external prevents him), shall do so when in some way activated—until then remaining inactive.

In another passage, the philosopher underlines two important attributes of knowledge. Whoever possesses *episteme* is able to think and study various subjects in their totality and can do that on his own free will as to when and how. There are parameters that differentiate knowledge—and thought generally—from sense-perception, contrary to what some other philosophers of those centuries believed. The Stagirite points to the differences clearly when he says that sense-perception is provoked by external stimuli (while thought is not) and the sensory experience deals with only a part of the sensory system—for example, vision, hearing, or other—while knowledge can theorize on the whole and examines a subject in its entirety. In addition, man can exercise his knowledge whenever he wants, in contrast to sense-perception, which does not depend upon himself, since a perceptible object must be present.

Opinion—doxa

Opinion is formed by the faculty of thought (*noein*), but is sometimes of doubtful credibility and is not always well established or of proven validity as knowledge is. Aristotle explains this position in an extensive discussion: Opinion may sometimes be true and at other times false because it does not entirely depend on us, since it is closely related to the senses. To prove that he brings the following example: Some things appear to us in a false way, although at the same time we have an ascertained and true conception (*upolepsis*) about them. For instance, the sun may look to an observer only one foot in diameter, while it is a fact that the sun is much bigger than the whole inhabited earth. So the observer has either to reject his opinion, or if he keeps it then his opinion is at the same time both true (for himself, subjectively) and wrong (in respect of reality).

In my view, the key word in the above syllogism is *upolepsis*, which is the only well-founded function that can lead to a correct conclusion corresponding to reality, since conception in the Aristotelian writings (and even today in modern psychophysiology) is the ultimate and of a higher-level faculty of thinking. That syllogism is also corroborated by a series of arguments in which the Stagirite contends that a convincing thought process can only exist in beings possessing the capability of reason (logic, *logos*). Opinion involves belief, he says, since one cannot have an opinion in which one does not believe; belief on the other hand is accompanied by conviction and one can only be convinced if logic intervenes. That is why, he continues, wild animals have no opinion or belief because they do not possess logic, although images may exist in them.

Aristotle with wide-range acuity comments on the factors that may influence the formation of opinion, as sometimes happens when it ends up incorrectly. As one such factor, he mentions emotional condition at a particular moment: when someone thinks something to be terrible or fearful (or conversely, thinks of something encouraging), he will feel a corresponding emotion, and in which case his opinion may be misled.

Prudent thinking (and acting)—phronesis

Phronesis (from the verb *phronein*) undoubtedly belongs to one of the types by which a thought process presents itself, but it has been used by the ancient philosopher in various places of the texts in different ways, so that most scholars have had difficulties in translating it. I have already mentioned that Aristotle in *On the Soul* uses in some passages *phronein* and *noein* interchangeably. At other places, *phronein* is a way by which conception (*upolepsis*) expresses itself, in a similar role with that it has in relation to thought (*nous*), when the latter is right in its content. (The term "understanding" is used by many translators.)

In the *Nicomachean Ethics* (Book VI 5, 7) there is a more analytic and elucidating description of the man possessing *phronesis*: he is the one who has the capacity to think well and deliberate deeply, in order to act rationally and prudently and achieve good life in general, as well as for a particular worthwhile end. So, apart from the process of thought being on the correct and logical track, in the definition of *phronesis* there is the element of an ability and push to action (*praxis*). In addition, an ethical connotation is evident when the philosopher remarks that a person with *phronesis* (a *phronimos*, in ancient and modern Greek) calculates well in matters good or bad for man. Furthermore, in the same chapter of the *Nicomachean Ethics* it is clearly stated that "prudence (*sophrosune*) saves *phronesis*", meaning that whoever has *phronesis* is prudent enough to know limitations and to exert self-control without any strain. In view of the above, I prefer to translate *phronesis* in a periphrastic way: prudent thinking-and-acting—instead of by one single word (for example, "understanding") which recognizes only one dimension of the ancient meaning.

Aristotle openly shows the moral parameter of *phronesis* in his argumentation, after which he declares it a virtue (although among the "intellectual" ones); that is the reason it is not corrupted or destroyed by pleasure or pain. Even more, it is a personality characteristic (*hexis*) that is improved by experience during the passing of years. So old people, according to the philosopher, have better ways to act in everyday problems; in this, prudent thinking is very close to *doxa* in old age (right opinion, then). It is also stressed that *phronesis* is not simply a rational characteristic or a trained ability, because in that case it would be affected by forgetfulness, while as a virtue it is not.

Prudent thinking-and-acting is divided by Aristotle into various categories according to the field in which it is applied. He distinguishes economic *phronesis*, the one dealing with household management, from the political, which has as its concern the affairs of the state, and then further divides the latter into legislative, judicial, and so forth.

Additional kinds of thought processes, as presented by the Stagirite, can be considered "choice" (*proairesis*) and "deliberation" (*vouleusis*), which we will discuss in the Section "Freedom of choice and decision".

Relation to other functions

Aristotle, in his work *On the Soul*, relates almost all other functions to that of thought. In its usual form as "thinking" (*nous*) or as "intellectual potentiality" (*dianoia*) it gives the proper direction to other faculties, so that a person can form a syllogism and reach to a conclusion, while as "logical thinking" (*logos, logisticon*) thought helps in checking whether a conclusion is right or wrong, true or false.

We have already discussed how thought is interdependent with sense-perception and imagination. At various points the Stagirite stresses the fact that thinking is based on images which remain in the place of percepts. He says: "Through images, as if seeing things, one can deliberate and decide about the future regarding the present" (431b). Nevertheless, he underlines the important role of logic as having the last word and warns us against the deceptions of imagination: "We cannot identify imagination with any of the faculties which are always right, like (scientific) knowledge and thought, since there exists also false imagination" (428a).

Regarding judgement, Aristotle is clear in his position when he states that it is the result of two processes, those of sense-perception and of intellectual thinking; at another point he adds prudent thinking. As the basis for correct judgement, he again considers sense-perception and some types of thought, following a question he himself puts as to whether we possess a function or a personality trait by which we come to truth or error; his answer includes right opinion and (scientific) knowledge.

The philosopher relates the faculty of psychomotor behaviour to thought mainly as regards one parameter—that of logical direction which thought provides to movements, so that a person is not drifted by his (instinctual) appetites or his imagination. The Stagirite compares some individuals who are influenced by their imagination in spite of their knowledge with what happens in animals, which do not possess logical thinking, and concludes that the two opposing forces regarding movement from place to place are correct thoughts and insatiable appetites.

Volition (will) according to Aristotle is a faculty presented in three types: wish (*voulesis*), desire (*epithumia*), and appetite (*orexis*). We will discuss these in detail in Chapter Four, but reference should be made here to their relation to thought and especially logical thinking. A general and persistent position of the philosopher is that wish always follows logic, while desire and appetite as a rule do not: When a person is acting according to wish, he is doing so within rational limits, but if he proceeds following his desires then he finds himself in the non-logical (*a-logon*) area. In contrast to wish, desire is an incessant seeking for pleasure and is opposed to logical thinking. That is why, the philosopher adds, morally weak people succumb to desire. There is an epigrammatic and laconic phrase of his in *On the Soul*: "Reason (*logos*) and desire run contrary to each other" (433b).

To appetites, Aristotle attributes intense and impulsive tendencies for satisfaction, "because above all it is the desirable object of appetite which originates a process (a movement) through thought and imagination" (433b). So appetites act against logic (which is always right), and appetites (like imagination) may often be wrong. To prove that logic still possesses the final decision on a subject, the philosopher reminds us that appetites are not dominant in morally strong people, who in spite of temptations do not act according to their desires but who, rather, follow reason.

It is psychologically noteworthy that the Stagirite's argumentation about desire-appetite on the one hand and logical thinking on the other is very close to how today we understand psychic conflict—the struggle between subconscious, impulsive drives

(Id) and defensive, prohibiting (Ego) mechanisms (see more in the section "Intrapsychic conflicts" in Chapter Eleven). One may find similarities also between the hedonistic nature of desire according to Aristotle and the psychoanalytic "pleasure principle", as well as between the rational thinking on any subject by *logos* (which is always correct) and the "reality principle" of psychoanalysis.

The ability to judge

Judgement according to a psychological definition is the function by which man, based on his knowledge, has the capacity to discriminate and compare things, ideas, and so forth, in order to choose between the essential and the unimportant, the true and the false, the useful and the useless, and so on. In a single phrase, Aristotle expresses the same qualities: "Judgement is the work of sense-perception and thought" (432a). So using two words, *aesthesis* and *dianoia*, he indicates the basis (sense-perception) through which man receives information, how then the latter is processed by intellectual thinking, with the end result being the ability to judge. In another chapter of *On the Soul*, he also mentions prudent thinking and opinion as helping us to know and discriminate between things and creatures in the world.

Judgement is influenced by imagination the Stagirite remarks, that is, by mental representations that remain in the mind after the stimuli cease to activate the sensory organs. At the same time, he very well knows that "the senses are always present (in accordance with the stimuli), while images are not" (428a). So the senses are all the time showing the reality of objects, but imagination may often not. As a result, the philosopher expresses his doubts as to whether one judging under the influence of imagination can be correct and not wrong. In that case, he says, previous opinions and (scientific) knowledge come to one's assistance. By accepting opinions (*doxa*) as basic in judgement, he indirectly admits that emotional conditions may also influence the final decision, but he does not openly state that in *On the Soul*.

In spite of the connection Aristotle presents between judgement and some types of thought which are of a purely psychic nature, he continues his discussion on a more (we would say) biological and psychophysiological basis. That happens because of his conviction that the senses are always true, and so he continues his argumentation as follows: Each one of the senses perceives the corresponding perceptible objects, is based on a particular sensory organ, and discriminates the differences between objects; for example, vision discriminates white from black, and taste discriminates sweet from bitter.

With his broad way of examining phenomena, the ancient philosopher raises the question: How can we at a certain moment judge correctly in case an object bears dissimilar qualities, that is, qualities perceptible by different sensory organs? His answer indicates a unifying process (or even organ?): "Discrimination of white and sweet cannot be effected by two different agencies; both qualities discriminated must be obvious to (conceived by) 'something' that is one and single" (426b). In this way, I believe, the Stagirite brings the issue to an upper level and to a process co-ordinating sensations arriving from different sensory organs. In the same chapter, he concludes, "what judges must be one, undivided and inseparable" (427a), and yet that "one" (*en*) when active at a single moment in time is capable of discriminating two or more separate qualities. It seems that the ancient philosopher by following his own syllogisms was at the end seeking a specific co-ordinating organ, which we today know is the brain, but about which in his era he could not have the right medical information.

CHAPTER FOUR

Volition (will) and psychomotor function

Volition is accepted today in psychological circles to be the function by which a person consciously chooses the planning and performing of a certain action. We can consider as equivalent to that what Aristotle calls "the appetitive part of the soul" (432b), in which he includes wish (*voulesis*), desire (*epithumia*), and appetite (*orexis*). He says that these form a faculty distinct from the others he enumerates, in respect of both reason and potentialities.

Wish

In Book III of *On the Soul* the philosopher proceeds to a differentiation by stating that wish has at its disposal the calculative abilities of logic, while desire and appetites (as well as passion) are characterized by irrational thinking. In our discussion about thought and imagination we have seen some parameters of their relation to volition. "Contrary to appetites and desires which are ignoring logic, wish always follows *nous*" (432b), that is, a right way of syllogisms, since *nous* represents a total of thought processes functioning correctly and according to reality. Wish, in addition, is not determined in its choices by imagination because, we were told, the latter can be true but it may be false.

Aristotle goes on to examine the origin of the volitional processes. He comes to the conclusion that there must exist an object of appetite (*orecton*), that is, a desirable target, in order for any such process to get started. That object is considered by far the most powerful motive, which instigates man to use any kind of thoughts and images in order to reach his scope. The philosopher remarks that every desirable object is not necessarily good (*agathon*), but it may simply seem to be good because of its forceful tendency for satisfaction. What is "good" and "not good" does not fall within the limits of the present discussion, given that it is a more philosophical issue. However, the Stagirite gives us two pieces of advice psychologically useful in order to avoid making mistakes. First, we should examine and observe what is applicable to the occasion; second, we should use a correct sequence of syllogisms.

Wish steadily follows such a sequence in accordance with the rules of logic. Unlike imagination, which is not always in a position to form well-based opinions, wish involves opinions based on sound inferences leading to decisions. In Chapter Eleven we will discuss some more details about the close relation of wish (*voulesis*) and two important processes—deliberation (*vouleusis*) and choice (*proairesis*)—which come to the assistance of man for consciously taking the right decisions and planning his performance. It is obvious (and remarkable) that the parameters the ancient philosopher attributes to wish are very similar to those of volition's definition according to modern psychology (mentioned earlier).

The different direction that a volitional act obtains depending on whether it proceeds accepting the rules of logic or not is presented by Aristotle in the conflict he describes between wish and appetite. Sometimes, he says, wish by applying reason overcomes appetite, while at other times appetite with its illogical and impulsive force overpowers wish. He even adds that different kinds of appetite may struggle one against the other. The philosopher's penetrating observation of intrapsychic dynamics is completed by a characterological description: Temperate people are motivated by wishes, but others who are carried away by appetites demanding immediate satisfaction lose self-control and become prodigal.

Aristotle quite aptly connects volitional behaviour with the ability of a person to have a proper sense of time. Persons taking consideration of what may happen in the future have wishes based on rational thinking and they hold back, while those full of desires are influenced by whatever satisfies them at that moment. For the latter such person "a pleasant object which is just at hand presents itself as both pleasant and good, without any condition, because of want of foresight into what is farther away in time" (433b).

Desire and appetite

Desire and appetite are not included on the list of mental functions in modern psychiatric reports. Some of the qualities the ancient philosopher attributes to desire and appetite are already obvious from what has been discussed a little before.

By desire, Aristotle denotes the process that starts upon the appearance of a pleasurable object. He expresses that in a laconic phrase: "Desire is the appetitive seeking of sweet pleasure" (414b). In this, it differs from wish and rational thinking; we were told that reason and desire "run contrary to each other" (433b). It has also been said to us that desire pushes a person towards a quick satisfaction at the present time, without any postponement for a more thoughtful examination of the final outcome and the consequences. The Stagirite is very clear on this: "He who acts in accordance with desire is an unrestrained man" (433a).

In contrast to wish, which throughout the text is considered a purely mental function, desire carries also a biological connotation. That becomes evident in the following passage: "Hunger and thirst are also desires, hunger for dry and hot, thirst for liquid and cold" (414b).

Appetite (*orexis*) is in most respects similar to desire, having the same main characteristic of acting irrespective of logic. Aristotle stresses the fact that appetite, by moving against any rational thinking, is often wrong, as is the case in actions based on images. Apart from that, it is significant that he attributes to appetite a more archaic quality, saying that "it is by nature a higher faculty and always more authoritative giving rise to other processes" (434a). So actually he considers it a primary, internal power actively directing the living creatures. The following passage is clear about it: "Appetite is an active process, with energy, giving a direction towards what it desires (towards the *orecton*); and that which is (basically) motivated and directed is the animal" (433b). So, in addition, a biological, instinctual quality is attributed to appetite.

In view of the above, I am of the opinion that *orexis* in the Aristotelian writings is equivalent to the psychoanalytic notion of instinctual drive. It is an innate function with great impetus and consists of instinctual tendencies expressing internal needs, which ask for immediate satisfaction at any cost, in an impulsive way. As a consequence, appetite, in order to reach its scope, activates other processes through the soul or/and the body. There is a noteworthy psychobiological (we would say today) approach of the ancient philosopher in Book III of *On the Soul*: "The instrument which appetite employs to produce a move is bodily; hence the examination of it falls within the province of the functions common to body and soul" (433b).

In spite of appetite's potentialities, we have seen when discussing thought that logic is able to overpower appetitive demands in people possessing self-control and high moral standards.

Although all schools agree that in the Corpus Aristotelicum there are some vague or even contradictory references for various subjects, I personally believe on the basis of our discussion up to now that regarding Volition we can sum up Aristotle's ideas in a series as follows: (a) Appetite (*orexis*) is an innate, instinctual drive, seeking satisfaction bodily or mentally, even in an irrational way; (b) Desire (*epithumia*) is produced upon the appearance of a pleasurable object and it acts in a hedonistic way, ignoring logic; and (c) Wish (*voulesis*) intervenes into the intentions of the above two and directs an action within reasonable limits.

Psychomotor activities

Psychomotor behaviour is an important part of man's life and a manifestation of one's personality and mental condition. Usually during psychological and psychiatric examinations the movements of the whole body, as well as those of groups of muscles (especially the facial), are observed and taken into consideration for writing the final report. Aristotle considers psychomotor behaviour a separate function, but he restricts his description in movements of a person from place to place (*kinesis kata topon*), in locomotion; he only here and there refers to other movements on the occasion of speaking about the behaviour during certain emotional conditions. The Stagirite enumerates psychomotor faculty among other generally recognized faculties at various points in *On the Soul*. He mentions psychomotor faculty together with sense-perception, appetite, thought, and nutrition, stating that only the latter, nutrition, exists in plants. At another point, he underlines the fact that it is "the soul" which activates movement ("psychomotor") in animals.

The philosopher, asking himself what it is that originates forward movement in an animal, links such a movement with imagination and appetite. There is always an end, he says, for an animal to move to, whenever it has an impulse to pursue or to avoid an object—except on those occasions when it is compelled to act in a certain way. He accepts, therefore, a purposeful intention of Nature, which provided animals with the advantage of moving from place to place, either in order to satisfy their desires, or to run away from a danger.

Examining the relation of psychomotor with other functions in man, Aristotle concludes that in addition to the innate impulses of appetite, man is in an advantageous position, having at his disposal the capacities of thought to direct his movements. In spite of that, he observes, many men are activated by their imagination, a process the philosopher presumably considers not dependable, since he remarks that all animals other than man possess no calculative thinking, but only imagination.

Movements expressive of emotional conditions are only sporadically found in the works of Aristotle. In *Problemata XXX* (which is attributed to the Aristotelian school but not to the philosopher himself) there is mention of the fact that people in fear are trembling. The condition of men getting drunk is also described—how they become joyful and move around, become insulting or even aggressive, with erotic intentions, and so on. The picture is compared to what happens in manic patients (who are thought to be under the influence of hot black-bile); they too are overactive, restless, extremely talkative, and easily moved by their passions and desires. The scene given in the text for the melancholics (literally "with black-bile", cold in their case) is different; they remain largely sluggish and inactive and when they move they do so in order to hang themselves! In *On Memory* Aristotle regards people of melancholic temperament as being inactive because they are annoyed at their inability to concentrate.

In the philosopher's *Rhetoric* (Book II), there is an excellent characterological comparison of young and old persons. The young, among other good and bad qualities, are described as all the time on the move, full of desires, and hot-blooded (*dia-thermoi*) "as if full of wine" (1389a). That is why they are easily excited, ready to fight, carried away by anger, and often insulting; on the other hand, they are humorous and pass their days laughing with their friends or indulging in sexual affairs. Old people are presented as the contrary—slow moving, unresponsive, sometimes frozen by fear. They are, as a rule, sad, but may have abrupt, albeit weak, outbursts.

CHAPTER FIVE

Affect (mood)

The emotional condition that bears the term "affect" or "mood" in psychology and psychiatry is not dealt with by Aristotle in *On the Soul* to the extent that one would expect. In a few passages he uses the word *thym-ikon*, which in modern Greek even today means "emotional disposition" and the root of which is met in many other languages; for example, in English, "dysthymia", "hypothymia", and "athymia". The philosopher does not analyse the content of the term *thym-ikon*, nor does he bring any examples, while he connects it with *epi-thymia*, that is, desire, by saying that in both states man is seeking pleasure. Of course, to some degree it is true that the mood is usually searching for something pleasurable and that man's emotional condition moves between opposite poles: pleasure–displeasure; joy–sadness; love–hate. Aristotle comments on the reactions to such conditions by saying that man, depending on the situation, will either proceed and pursue or avoid and leave (an equivalent to the modern psychophysiological rule of fight-or-flight).

In the first chapter of Book I of *On the Soul* the Stagirite enumerates quite a few emotions under the heading *pathe* (usually translated into "affections" or, better, into "experiences, phenomena of the soul"): joy, sorrow, courage, fear, calmness, pity, love, hate, anger. However, the work in which the philosopher examines in detail many affects (calling them again *pathe*) is Book II of the *Rhetoric*. There he elaborates extensively on the emotional disposition of men under certain conditions, who and what provokes such a reaction, in favour or against whom the emotion is directed, and so on, giving also some psychodynamic interpretations.

Here I will only briefly mention the description that Aristotle gives for a few emotions. He starts with a definition of *pathe* as "all those which by changing the (emotional) disposition of men affect their judgement, and then pleasure or displeasure follows" (1378a).

Anger is characterized by Aristotle as the emotion of somebody who has been hurt and whose behaviour is punishing and vengeful. This happens when the individual is annoyed and vexed because of the humiliating actions of others, and who hence reacts with anger or revenge, so that in his imagination he feels comfort and pleasure.

Calmness is defined by Aristotle as the opposite of anger and as characteristic of meek people. Any mature person will remain calm in front of those who show a serious behaviour and do not confront him with contempt, but express their respect.

Fear is discussed by the philosopher from the point of view of those who may provoke fear and of whom one should be cautious. Worse are the persons who have power and behave unjustly to the weak and poor, as well as those who are contemptuous and cunning.

Courage is produced under certain conditions, and the Stagirite's comments show an almost psychodynamic approach. One becomes courageous, he says, after having gone through various misfortunes without having been hurt. He brings the example of sailors who feel full of courage when they have survived a terrible storm and are confident how to sail from now on. Ignorance may also lead to courage those who have never come across heavy seas and who may, as a result, risk their ship and their lives in spite of warnings.

Pity is the sadness and sympathy one feels for somebody who is suffering many painful experiences, while he deserves a better life. This, the philosopher explains, is felt even more if one thinks that similar sufferings may happen to him or his dear ones. Nemesis, on the other hand, is the justified anger and indignation against somebody who is unworthy of the prosperous and happy life he enjoys.

(Nemesis was usually mentioned as a divine punishment by the Gods for insulting people.)

Aristotle's ability to make subtle differentiations between complex emotional states in simple words is remarkable. Envy is defined by the philosopher as the annoying feeling one has when somebody equal to him is much more fortunate, while his own life remains without any improvement. Jealousy is again a displeasure when a worthy man sees others around him happy; but this affect instigates him for further efforts and initiatives without bad feelings against anyone.

CHAPTER SIX

Memory

The process of memory

Many schools of psychology and psychophysiology today accept that the sensory organs when activated produce percepts, which then remain in the mind as mental representations—visual, auditory, and so on. We have seen that Aristotle describes a very similar process and calls such a mental representation a *phantasma*—"image", according to an Oxford translation. The Greek word comes from a Homeric verb meaning "to appear", "to be seen"—so in fact the philosopher means mainly something which had been seen, and then kept in "imagination" (*phantasia*) as an image. He underlines this visualization when he states that one cannot think or understand without images. He further clarifies such a connection of thought and images by saying that thinking proceeds by using "pictures", "impressions", or "written words" (*graphe*).

Aristotle in all his works gives great importance to the senses, to which he also devotes a separate book (*Sense and Sensibilia*). Regarding memory, he points to sense-perception (*aesthesis*) as the primary function, which through the formation of images constitutes the basis for thinking and for memory. In his treatise *On Memory*, he specifically writes: "Memory only incidentally belongs to the function of thought, but essentially it belongs to the function of sense-perception" (450a). In order to support his view he adds that if memory were a function exclusively of thought, it would not be found in many animals possessing no thinking abilities.

Today many psychologists speak of imageless-thinking in addition to other types, but the Stagirite of the 4th century B.C. wanting to stress the role of sense-perception stated that "even memory of abstract thoughts involves an image" (450a).

Aristotle has commented on another interesting parameter necessary for memory to be produced—that of time. He believes that memory is not simply sense-perception, nor only cognitive-conception, but a function related to both after a lapse of time. Consequently, only animals which perceive time are capable of remembering. In addition, he adds in an explicit (and almost poetic) way: "For the present only sense-perception is needed, for the future hope and for the past memory—so any memory implies passing of time (*meta chronou mneme*)" (449b).

The philosopher also introduces another element in the process of memorizing—that of quantity and/or size. He observed that man cannot imagine an object without thinking of it in terms of quantity. Even for objects without definite size or quantity in one's mind, the image is formed in terms of those elements. So, according to the Stagirite, a proper memory cannot exist without a sense of time, of quantity, and size. It is in man's nature and ability to envisage objects in that way.

The phases of the whole process of memory have been described by Aristotle in a way similar in most aspects to that which have been taught by many courses of Descriptive Psychology during the last century, while some of his observations can be found in theories of today's Dynamic Psychology.

The first stage of the process starts when an external stimulus activates a sensory organ, in which case an image is produced and, as the Greek philosopher puts it, "the soul (the mind) conceives a picture or a thought" (450b). The importance for memory lies in the fact that the image "is imprinted (is stamped), like when we seal with the stone of a ring" (450a). Therefore, *imprinting* is the ultimate result of the first phase, and in that way a number of images are produced in the human mind. The second phase is that of *retention* of the images for a period—retained according to (as we saw) the size of an object, the chronological point of a happening, and so forth.

When one studies carefully the works of Aristotle, one will notice that subjects relevant to imprinting and retaining, and therefore to memory, are to be found in many other treatises of his. For instance, in his work *On Dreams* he states that the effect of a stimulus continues to exist even when the stimulus has departed and is no more affecting. He explains this by assuming that "actual perceiving is a qualitative and enduring change (*alloiosis*) in the organism" (459b)—a change analogous to what psychologists in recent years called "memory trace". At the same time, he specifically says that "the day's processes of the senses are repressed" (460b) and that they remain "latent, in depth in the mind" (463a). These are views that one using modern terminology could call neurophysiological on the one hand, or even psychodynamic on the other. In general, one is impressed by the psychobiological (as we would today say) approach of the ancient philosopher. In his work *On Sleep*, he concludes: "What is called sense-perception is an active process of the soul (*psyche*) through the body (*soma*)" (454a).

Recollection

In order for the process of memory to be completed, after imprinting and retention a third phase is necessary—that of *recollection*. Aristotle defines recollection as the activity by which one is reminded and recovers the knowledge, perceptions, and experiences that he had before. He further explains how this operation takes place: When we recollect we are trying to "hunt" the next event in a series (in association), so we start from the present, or the similar, or the contrary, or something near to what we seek. Such an associative process is better shown in an example which the philosopher brings: "Some people have better memory because they associate more quickly: If they try to remember a season of the year and they happen to see some milk, their mind goes to white, from white to fog, from fog to humidity, so humidity reminds them of the autumn, which they were trying to remember" (452a). The similarity with free-association which goes on at the analytic couch when the psychoanalyst asks the patient to speak freely whatever comes into his mind, so that useful material can emerge from the subconscious, is more than obvious (and remarkable!).

The associative searching may, according to Aristotle, be active or, at other instances, non-active. He underlines the fact that of all animals only man is able to actively recollect, because an inference (a process of syllogisms [*syllogismos*]) is needed; that is, whatever a man saw or heard or suffered, he later thinks about it deeply and so an operation of investigation starts for recalling it. The non-active process that the philosopher describes is very interesting. He says, for example, that sometimes, without any effort, a certain memory just suddenly enters into our mind (a name; a song), because by habit or experience it had been associated (unconsciously, we may explain today) with something else similar to what is happening. The Stagirite himself indicates such a subconscious process when, in another passage, he notes: "The way various facts in life are related to each other in a sequence (in a series), in the same way they are internally kept for memory" (451b).

Another sequential association is presented by Aristotle in an example of alphabetical letters he provides in *On Memory*:

(past) A B C D E F G H I (recent)

If one tries to remember A, he may first remember E, and then memory direction to D or F is easier, and from D to C—B and so on to A (452a).

The discussion about memory gives Aristotle the opportunity to raise a philosophical and, for psychiatrists, a psychophysiological, issue: How is it that when we perceive the image in our mind, in our soul comes the real (although absent) thing? Why is it that a picture or word imprinted in our mind brings us a relevant memory and that we feel (as if directly seeing) the real thing? The ancient philosopher brings the following example: An animal painted on a vase is both a picture and (for us) a certain animal—both an *icon* and a *zoon*. In addition, he continues giving himself the answer: "That is effected by the ability of the soul (the mind) to process a memory and give meaning to objects for us" (451a).

Memory disturbances

Aristotle did not write any separate chapter on the disturbances of memory, but there are various references on such conditions which can be collected from several of his treatises, and which show his acute ability to observe even clinical phenomena. Before commenting on those, let us see some interesting descriptions by the philosopher of memory deflections happening in everyday life. For instance, he mentions how we are sometimes in doubt as to whether something occurring in our mind is really a memory or not and if we ever actually had in the past a perception that corresponds to it. He also describes the phenomenon during which, while trying to remember a name, we may blunder onto a similar one we happen to know and say that one instead. The Stagirite explains such wrong recollections by believing that at times "an impulse in the mind moves" (450b) the process not in the required direction, but otherwise. In addition, since he generally accepts the case of accidental occurrences contrary to nature, in the same way memories, he says, may happen *by chance.*

The wide range of interests of the philosopher would not leave out *psychopathological phenomena.* He describes the condition during which occasionally one sees an object and gets the idea that one saw or heard of it formerly, while actually one did not. The explanation given is that sometimes mental contemplation of an object may regard it incorrectly, as relative to some other and not the real one. Such an experience is very similar to what today we call *déjà vu.*

In *On Memory* Aristotle mentions the case of certain persons "mentally deranged" (presumably *hallucinating psychotics*), "who spoke of their (hallucinated) images as facts of their past experience, and are remembering them as such" (459a). He also points to *old age dementia* when he repeatedly refers to the elderly being defective in memory (*amnemon*). The reasons he gives are very interesting; he states that old people are in decay, that they have become mentally too slow, and that images are not imprinted at all—"the images do not even touch their soul" (450b). This viewpoint coincides with today's clinical knowledge that demented people are forgetful regarding recent events (that have not been imprinted), while they still preserve memories of many years before.

Aristotle gives great importance, as we saw, to the senses, particularly during the first stages of the process of memory. In *On Dreams*, he discusses the effects of emotions on sense-perception, and as a consequence on memory. He describes cases in which, because of the emotional condition one lives at a certain moment (waiting for a friend; fearing an enemy is coming; being in love, etc.), sense-perception is easily deceived and the impression left in memory is incorrect. In the treatise *On Memory*, he specifically says: "In those strongly moved owing to passion, no memory is formed" (450b). In other passages, he mentions similar conditions when one is excited by anger or lives in fear; so actually he spoke of *anxiety states*. On the other hand, he accepts that emotion may play a positive role in imprinting and retaining, when he writes that sometimes a single experience may affect somebody more deeply, so as to remember it better than others that he has lived or seen frequently.

Affective disorders are described in a small book entitled *Problemata XXX*, which is attributed by some scholars to Aristotle, although many others think it belongs to a pupil of the Stagirite, written many years later. The symptomatology of *depression* (*melancholia*) is presented in detail, with terms that are in use internationally today: *hypothymia, dysthymia, athymia*, as well as "sadness", "inactivity", "pessimism", "suicidal tendencies", and so forth. In addition, the opposite condition of *mania* is described very aptly: *hyperthymia*, talkativeness, erotic manifestations, overactivity, aggressiveness, and so on. Nevertheless, in that text there is no mention of any memory difficulties.

In another short book (which definitely was written by Aristotle), *On Divination of Sleep*, there is reference to a psychopathology of the "insane" that indirectly ends up in wrong recollection. The author portrays manic persons (*manicoi*) as impetuous and constantly changeable with a quick series of thoughts in their mind that leads to incorrect memory. He gives as an example the case of such a person reciting a poem and saying "-phrodite" instead of "Aphrodite" (464b). In a passage of the same book the ancient philosopher (perhaps noticing the bipolarity of the condition?) states: "The natural temperament of the garrulous and the melancholic is such that they may see visions of all types" (463b).

Aristotle in his book *On Memory*, his main study on the subject, is more explicit and explanatory about what happens in depressed people regarding recollection: "Some persons have become unable to recollect in spite of their trying to concentrate and they feel discomfort—they then abandon their effort, especially persons of melancholic temperament" (453a).

CHAPTER SEVEN

Consciousness—dreams

Consciousness is disturbed in various psychiatric conditions and so it is necessary for the examiner to evaluate its level during psychological testing or psychiatric diagnosing. Being awake does not always mean that somebody is conscious enough of the surroundings and of himself, and sufficiently alert and ready to accept stimuli, to concentrate and respond. Aristotle in his treatise *On Sleep* of his book *Parva Naturalia* deals with the subject more by discussing wakefulness than directly about consciousness.

In some cases, he is more exact; he describes loss of consciousness in persons who have fainted or have received blows to the neck. He also refers to epilepsy as characterized by loss of consciousness similar in a way to that of sleep. Otherwise, he clearly states that sleep is a different condition than disturbances in which there is unconsciousness of the form seen in asphyxia, or when a person falls into a deep trance and is considered dead. In such cases, the perceptive faculty is extremely weakened, and although—the philosopher correctly comments—one may sometimes see images and speak about them when in a trance, that experience is not a dream.

Starting to examine the subject of wakefulness and sleep the ancient philosopher puts a series of questions which he proceeds to answer in a psychobiological (we today would say) way: Are they manifestations of the body or the soul, or both? What is their purpose? Is there any usefulness? What happens during dreaming?

The main position of Aristotle is that sleep (*hypnos*) and wakefulness, which he sees as a state of being conscious and alert, are directly dependent on the function of sense-perception regarding both external and internal stimuli (as we will see when discussing dreams). He points to the fact that plants do not possess the function of sleeping and waking because they do not have sensory organs, but only organs for growing. Based on his view that "sense-perception is a process of the soul through the body" (454a), the ancient philosopher gives a psychobiological explanation (very close to modern theories) that sleep is an active (*energeia*) phenomenon which does not involve only the psyche but also the body; "on the other hand a soulless body is not able to feel (and be conscious)" (454a).

In the text of *On Sleep*, there are significant comments on the expediency and usefulness of sleep. The Stagirite begins with a general principle that Nature always operates for the sake of a definite goal and that goal is a good one (*agathon*). He brings the parallel example of every creature endowed by Nature with the ability to move, which nevertheless cannot forever and continuously move because it gets tired; so rest is necessary and beneficial. In a similar way Man, as any animal, cannot incessantly act and needs rest obtained through sleep.

According to the philosopher, sleep's purpose is for all animals to be saved and preserved in good condition; in the case of Man a waking healthy state is the goal, during which he can think and feel properly—"the ultimate and best goal for Man" (455b). In order to reinforce his argument of the waking, conscious condition being a tiring and consuming action, Aristotle gives us another example: the eyes get tired if seeing for a long period of time and have to stop doing so and close, like all organs "which Nature has at our disposal must weaken their efforts when they have surpassed the time for which they can work" (454b). Another beneficial effect of sleep for all animals, according to the philosopher, is that while it lasts nutrition and growth are especially promoted.

It is interesting that Aristotle proceeds to consider the physiology of sleep and, for that, he follows the restricted existing knowledge of his era—in terms of hot–cold, liquid–solid, and so on. He adopts the view that the food turned into "exhalations" (vapours) enters the vessels and, hot as they are, the blood carries them to the upper part of the body where they are cooled and again descend (like the vapours of sea water ascending and becoming clouds and then descending as rain). That is why, the Stagirite explains, it is after meals that sleep comes since the hot "exhalations" produce heaviness in the head and the eyelids drop, like when one takes wine or poppy. As soon as digestion is completed, wakefulness and clear consciousness return.

The origins of dreams

In *On Dreams* Aristotle shows his remarkable (psychodynamic, I would say) ability of approaching intrapsychic phenomena. He first examines which faculties are involved in the creation of dreams. As with other phenomena, he considers that sense-perception has a primary role in this, but he still wonders: How is it that a person during dreaming sees images, although he is not conscious of his environment at that time and vision is not active? Therefore, at the end, in order to explain the phenomenon he accepts that at least three functions are involved: sense-perception, consciousness, and imagination. Nothing can happen, he states, if one has not previously (while awake and conscious) seen an object, so that sense-perception can actively produce its image (as the material for the dream).

Furthermore, the philosopher observes that two more functions may be a part of dreaming. First, there is thought, since there is the example of many people who remember that during sleeping—in their dreams, or irrespective of them—they settled various problems and formed logical solutions. Second, there is judgement, which if weakened and incorrect will lead to irrational and distorted dreams (as we shall later discuss).

About the origins and final formation of dreams, Aristotle, in his works *On Dreams* and *On Divination of Sleep*, presents astonishingly interesting theories which are in agreement with many aspects of modern psychophysiological and psychodynamic knowledge. As we saw in the discussions about imagination and memory, the philosopher in the same way considers sense-perception as the fundamental faculty for the whole process of dreaming. He insists on the property of that faculty to accept stimuli, which "through the resulting phenomenon" (459a) leave a continuing effect on the organism even when they cease to act. As a striking example, he brings an observation from everyday life: When we transfer our gaze from the sunlight to darkness (or if we close our eyes), the feeling of something shining still persists. Likewise, if we look long at one object in one colour, for example, green, and then we look at another object, that one also seems to us green.

In addition to the resulting effect, the continuation of which we are allowed to assume consists of images (according to what has already been exposed by Aristotle), the philosopher presents the theory of propagation of stimuli and of the phenomena that follow: that which sets a process, excites movement in another part nearby, he says, and that propagates onward. This "movement" is described as a qualitative (and even structural) change (*alloiosis*) and in the text, there is the following comparative example: "Something heated by a hot object heats what is next to it and the transmission is continuous" (459b).

Aristotle proceeds to the next step concerning the formation of dreams. He explicitly states that propagation of perceptual phenomena is directed into "the deeper parts" (459b) of the organism. And he explains how and why that happens: The philosopher generally accepts that the external and internal stimuli provoke processes which are at times either active or latent ("in a potential state") (463a). The latter occur in the case of some other processes based upon previous sensory impressions of the daytime, which if not strong enough (because the senses and the intellect are at work in an awake and conscious person) are pushed away—"like slight pleasures and pains which are extinguished by great ones for a while" (461a). At night during sleep, the opposite takes place; owing to the inaction of the senses and the intellect, the extruded phenomena (images) which have remained latent display themselves—become evident—as the manifest dream. The Stagirite insists on the energetic quality of intrapsychic phenomena during sleep: "The internal potential forces actualize themselves as soon as an impediment has been put away" (461b).

Considering the above, one, I think, is excused to point to a parallelism in a number of respects between Aristotle's theories and today's scientific knowledge: (a) Sense-perception and the resulting images are accepted also by modern psychology as the basic origin of most dreams; (b) Propagation of the processes reminds one of the excitation, we now know, from one neuron to another; (c) Extrusion of processes and images, as well as their retention in "the deeper parts" of the mind in a latent state is equivalent to what psychoanalysts would call repression into the unconscious; and (d) The manifest dream is comprised out of those repressed images.

Aristotle's ability to observe human phenomena in a clear, penetrating, and exact way provides the possibility for him to distinguish between dreams and some conditions during which a person is semi-conscious: He describes the hypnagogic phenomena with pseudohallucinations when one is entering into (or coming out of) sleep; a person can hear distant sounds or see a faint lamp during light sleep. Also it does not escape the attention of the philosopher that although as a rule one feels that whatever is taking place during dreaming is really happening, sometimes the person understands that he is at that very time asleep and dreaming.

It is not without significance that the effect of emotions on sense-perception is described by Aristotle in his text *On Dreams*, thus showing that the resulting images and hence the content of the dream is formed accordingly. Under the influence of fear, for instance, one has the illusion when seeing a stranger of seeing his enemy; under the influence of love, that he sees his beloved. The stronger the passion the more one is deceived, like in anger or in desire, the philosopher adds.

In his short treatise *On Divination of Sleep*, Aristotle is facing the subject with scientific impartiality, stating at first that the so-called prophetic ability of some persons cannot either be dismissed or be given confidence without previous detailed examination. He is prompted in this by the fact that "even charismatic physicians tell us that one should pay much attention to dreams" (463a). He, nevertheless, soon rejects the whole idea, including theocratic views of his time: "That God is sending prophetic dreams has no basis" (462b). And with some irony he says that it surpasses any logic and prudence for anyone to believe that he can foresee what will happen at the Pillars of Hercules (Gibraltar) or, at the other end of the earth, the banks of Borysthenes (the River Dnieper in Russia).

Dream and daytime actions

The ancient philosopher gives his own realistic explanation of how some dreams seem "prophetic". He distinguishes three types relating them to daytime actions. First, when during the day we are planning to do something or are already engaged in it, we may during sleep be concerned about it and continue to perform it in our dream. Second, thoughts that come up in the images of a dream may become starting points and pave the way for actions taken up during the next day; then it is wrongly considered that the dream has been fulfilled. Third, the same belief may be taken if, by mere coincidence, something seen in a dream then happens in the following days.

Apart from daytime actions affecting the content of dreams, Aristotle remarks that somatic or external stimuli may bring about relevant images in a dreamer. The example given is that of a slight warmth of the body which is felt in sleep as if the person is walking through fire, or that of a faint ringing in the ears, which is taken as thunder and lightning. (The same examples are described today in medicine and explained on a psychophysiological basis.)

Everyone has wondered at times how it is that the content of some dreams is easily recognized and understood, while that of others remains unrecognized and unintelligible. Psychoanalysis in modern years gives its own explanation. According to its theories, the latent thoughts and wishes can follow two roads during dreaming. In the first case, the latent wishes and impulses from the unconscious find their gratification in a visual form, that is, in the images of the manifest dream. So there happens a wish-fulfillment, easily recognized by the dreamer when he wakes up, since there is a clear and straight relationship between the latent and the manifest content. Aristotle's observing capability points out this very resemblance and also that "anyone can interpret these plain and 'straight' dreams" (*euthuoneiria*) (464b).

The other road, which the latent wishes quite often follow, may lead to an incomprehensible manifest dream. That happens, according to psychoanalysis, because the wishes are impermissible and objectionable, so that defence mechanisms oppose their direct representation in the manifest content; this intrapsychic intervention produces a disguise of the original images. Aristotle offers a very similar, "psychodynamic" interpretation, when he says that "the internal (emotional) processes efface the clearness of the dream" and it appears unrecognizable and "distorted" (*diestrammena*) (464b)—the very word that psychoanalysts use today! Those internal processes are described by the philosopher in a pictorial way: The distorted dream images are analogous to the forms reflected in the water of a lake—if there is a great motion in the water the reflection of objects has no more resemblance to the real objects. Aristotle ends his discussion with an interesting comment: "Skilful, indeed, would be in interpreting such reflections, he who could at a glance comprehend the distorted fragments of the forms—similarly then, of his dream and what it means" (464b).

CHAPTER EIGHT

Nutrition and reproduction

Nutrition and reproduction are enumerated by Aristotle in Book II of his work *On the Soul*, together and on the same line with basic mental functions (sensory, psychomotor, thought), while today we consider those two more as biological. Yet, in a broader sense, one can speak of them as psychosomatic—see, for instance, psychogenic anorexia, bulimia, and impotence.

The ancient philosopher explains his categorization on the fact that nutrition through food maintains life, and life exists in beings possessing a soul (he even coined the term "nutritive soul"). "Since nothing is fed which is not alive, the body which is fed is besouled—and that happens not by chance" (416b). He also remarks that nutrition is necessary from birth until death for everything that is alive. Without nutrition, it is impossible for a being to grow, mature and, lastly, decay. The Stagirite underlines the psychic power of nutrition, which continuously preserves a creature in order to remain the way that it is; food in addition prepares a being to act appropriately.

In spite of the inclusion of nutrition among the mental functions, it seems that Aristotle kept some reservations. At one point, he explicitly states that the faculty of self-nutrition could be separated from the rest, but not they from it. To that thought, he was led by the fact that "nutrition is the only 'psychic' potentiality which plants possess" (414a). We must not overlook the philosopher's position that all plants must be considered as living "for they show to have a primary power to increase and decrease in various directions ... and continue to live so long as they can absorb nutriment" (434a).

Aristotle differentiates very aptly the ontological from the phylogenetic purpose of Nature. Survival of the individual is accomplished by the process of nutrition, which involves three parts: the "nutritive soul" (415a) (equivalent to the hunger instinct?) initiating feeding; food which fulfils that need; and, third, a besouled body, which is fed and maintained. Perpetuation of the species is achieved by the "reproductive soul" (416b).

The philosopher proceeds to the following syllogism: The right way to approach anything is to examine whether it realizes its end (*telos*). The end in this case is for a being to generate another being like itself. Therefore, the first and foremost potentiality of the soul is the reproductive. The Stagirite elaborates furthermore: "For all normal living things the most natural action is to produce another like themselves—an animal to produce an animal and a plant a plant—so that they participate in the eternal and the divine, as far as they can; since that is what all desire and for the sake of that they do whatever they do, according to the rules of Nature ... and because no perishable being can remain alive eternally, it continues to exist in something like itself" (415a).

With his ideas in the above passage, Aristotle passes beyond the everyday facts of life to philosophical spheres and from there back to a human, psychological level. In an almost poetic phrase, he characterizes the birth of a child as giving Man the opportunity to fulfil an important wish and "participate in the eternal and the divine" (415a), to surpass death and unite with something immortal. At the same time, I think, that one can see the tragic aspect of life for Man, since even for that aim one has to obey and act strictly within the limits of the Laws of Nature—getting only a partial satisfaction through the creation of an offspring.

PART III

FORMATION OF THE PERSONALITY

A basic outline regarding the factors contributing to the formation of human personality is agreed by most "schools" of psychology and psychiatry. Of course, there are different views concerning certain topics of the long process of the individual towards maturity, but it is accepted by all that the main elements can be classified into three categories:

1. The first is the characteristics with which Nature endows Man, both somatic and psychic, from his birth onward, either as capabilities or as potentialities for further development. Some of them are what we medically call "hereditary" and others constitutional.
2. The second is the effects of the environment—natural and human—that are recognized to continuously affect the whole development of a person. From the very first days of childhood, the relations with parents and siblings are decisive for the formation of character, as well as later the relations with teachers and schoolmates, in adolescence with the opposite sex, in marital life with the husband/wife, and so on.

3. The third concerns how the Self of a person is formed from the interrelations of the above elements, direct or indirect, but also the significance that as one grows one's Self takes a more active part in the psychological processes, voluntarily or involuntarily, consciously or unconsciously.

The various "schools" seem to disagree on these last issues mainly, but closer study shows that essentially they do not totally reject the theories of others; rather, they each seek to underline their own viewpoint, for example, the unconscious processes or the learning theories or interpersonal relations.

Here I intend to examine the views of Aristotle concerning the formation of the personality, classifying them according to the three axes mentioned above, and, where possible, finding their similarities or differences corresponding to modern psychoanalytic theories.

CHAPTER NINE

The gifts of Nature

Aristotle was an untiring student of Nature in the broadest possible sense. By personal observation and introducing the empirical method in philosophy, he examined hundreds of plants and animals, as well as various phenomena of Nature, and so it was impossible not to connect the existence of Man with the latter. His approach and the animalistic qualities he attributes (along with the psychological) to the human being, led to what some call "naturalistic theorization", although it could equally be called biological.

The Stagirite expresses his admiration for the great power and wisdom of Nature in his treatise *On the Soul* with a phrase that has become standard: "Nature never does anything in vain (without a reason), nor does it leave out something necessary" (432b). With yet another phrase, complementary to the previous, he stresses the purposefulness of Nature: "All things in Nature exist for a certain aim" (434a), and that for every creature to reach its target the work of Nature is a prerequisite.

The philosopher points to the immense and multiform possibilities of Nature and their superiority compared to the abilities of Man. In the *Nicomachean Ethics*, in a discussion about happiness, he states that everything that depends on Nature is as good as it can be. In addition, in another passage, he claims that Nature is more exact and better than any human art. Regarding the personality he believes that it is more difficult to change the traits given by Nature, that is, the hereditary, than those that are built later in life (although he calls these "second Nature" [1152a]). Underlining the stability of Nature, he writes: "What comes from Nature remains and is universal, having the same force everywhere—like the fire which burns in the same way in Greece, as well as in Persia" (1134b).

In view of the above, the basic role that Aristotle attributes to Nature for the creation of life becomes evident. In *Physics*, he clearly says: "Nature is the cause for the existence of animals and their organs, in the same way as for plants and the simple elements—earth, fire, air and water" (192b). And in *On the Soul*: "The elements of Nature are the origin of all others—and among the latter some have life and the rest have not. By life we mean whatever can be fed, develops and perishes" (412a). The examples which the philosopher brings to illustrate the contribution of Nature to a proper functioning of man's body are scattered in many of his books. In *On the Soul*, for instance, he describes how Nature uses the tongue for both taste and speech; how air serves in both warming the body and producing voice.

Constitution and potentialities

In *Nichomachean Ethics* Aristotle is mainly concerned as to how Man can best obtain moral virtues, that is, the praiseworthy characteristics of the personality. What is, then, his opinion of the role of Nature in this process? At the beginning of Book II of that work he makes a statement which, if taken by itself, leads to a one-sided position: "No moral virtue is given to us by Nature" (1103a). He even brings examples of natural phenomena to show that they cannot be changed, like the stone which when dropped moves always downwards, or the fire which always burns upwards. Yet a few lines further on and in the same passage, obviously accepting that the physical laws are not always applicable in human psychology, he rephrases the above position: "Therefore, virtues do not develop in us by Nature nor contrary to Nature; rather we are equipped by Nature *to receive* them and then they are completed by habit" (1103a; my own emphasis). (We will later discuss the great significance that Aristotle attributes to habit, the effort of Man to obtain the right behaviour and life through better customary and repeated actions. The philosopher himself points to the fact that the word "habit" in Greek, that is, *ethos* is synonymous with ethical behaviour [*ethiki*].)

He furthermore clarifies that regarding whatever arises in us by Nature, first we are endowed with the potentialities (*dynameis*; see Part 2 "Mental functions") and then we can act accordingly. In *Metaphysics*, he considers some of the potentialities innate (*syggeneis*), for example, the senses, which we can use without previously having to get accustomed by habit. Nevertheless, he has also told us (see Chapter Two "Sense-perception") that the senses are fundamental for other, purely mental, functions like memory, imagination, and judgement, which differ from person to person.

If one puts the above views of Aristotle in a series, the conclusion is that: Nature provides the human being with basic qualities on which the personality can be built. An individual is receptive of the moral virtues by originally being equipped with functions which today we would call basically biological, like the senses, nutrition, and reproduction (see Chapter Eight "Nutrition and reproduction"); through those, following outer influences (Chapter Ten "The effects of the environment") and actions by different habits in each case (Chapter Eleven "The responsibility of one's Self"), a special personality profile is shaped. These views are in accordance with modern theories about individual constitutional traits on which different characteristics develop in each person.

Judgement, a purely mental function, is a good example of the processes mentioned above. According to Aristotle, "Judgement is the result of the senses and thought" (432a) (see Chapter Three "Thought and judgement"). Through the sensory system various stimuli from outside give us information which is processed by intellectual functions and, according to how well a person is endowed by Nature and the experience he obtains by habit or the emotional situations he has lived, a better or less correct judgement develops. So constitution and potentialities contribute in various indirect ways to the characteristics of personality.

Another illustrative example is the function of reproduction, the first and foremost potentiality, as Aristotle calls it, since every living thing desires to produce another like itself according to the rules of Nature. Reproduction is mainly a biological function of Nature, which pushes an individual to the opposite sex, and thus in an indirect way provides the opportunity of various interpersonal relations, with the ultimate result of enrichment of personality. For instance, the Stagirite stresses the fact that although two persons may first be only biologically attracted to each other, when they live as a couple new, purely psychological, qualities arise in them; they help and love each other, not merely for procreation. And he adds: "They even find joy in the virtues of the other partner" (1162a).

The philosopher also notes how Nature influences women to bear children and how then in motherhood new feelings are present, such as care and affection, which in mothers are stronger than in fathers. He nevertheless comments that Nature, through the same faculty, the reproductive, may lead to a different behaviour. As a paradigm, he refers to homosexuals, about whom he believes that for their sexual orientation in some cases Nature has been responsible, and in others it is because they were sexually abused during childhood.

Among the channels through which Nature indirectly affects the shaping of personality is the variety of interrelations of potentialities in each particular individual. There happen co-operations and conflicts between functions according to each person's intensity of desires, logical thinking, emotional disposition, and so forth. Aristotle in *On the Soul* describes such a conflict between appetites and desires on the one hand and rational thinking on the other. We have seen in the discussion about will (see Chapter Four "Volition [will] and psychomotor function") that appetites can be considered a psychobiological function equivalent in psychoanalytic terms to the instinctual drives. They seek immediate satisfaction in an impulsive and even irrational way. Desire also acts against any logic on the appearance of a pleasurable object. Depending on the prevalence of one or the other potentiality given by Nature—that is, instinctual tendencies or rational thinking—certain characteristics of the personality will be shaped. So those who resist temptations and do not act according to desires but instead follow logic become morally strong persons, while, as the philosopher says, those in whom reason is not dominant during a conflict but who rather follow their hedonistic desire, become unrestrained people.

Does Nature directly affect the personality?

Apart from the ways discussed above, does Nature directly affect the personality? The answer of Aristotle lies in Book II of the

Nicomachean Ethics, where he describes various types of human behaviour in his concern about how Man can acquire virtues. The philosopher's opinion is that Nature is responsible when Man is attracted more to whatever is distant to the "mean", which coincides with virtue. He specifically believes that "Nature made us" (*pephykamen*) (1109a) more inclined to pleasure, and therefore to self-indulgence and debauchery than decency and self-discipline. It is noteworthy that, like modern theories speak of constitutional differences from one person to another, Aristotle also states that the effects of Nature are different in each individual. In another chapter of the same book, he advises us to look and examine which traits are stronger in our personality, "since each one of us has by Nature tendencies towards other targets" (1109b); he also recommends that we can recognize these tendencies by observing the pleasure or pain we feel about them.

The above positions of individual differences by the ancient philosopher show once again that he was never dogmatic or absolute when he was dealing with human psychology. That is also evident in other passages of the *Nicomachean Ethics* in which he wants to demonstrate the direct effect of Nature on the personality in the case of acts of uncontrolled behaviour; he at the same time admits, for instance, that in addition to somebody by Nature being brutal and acting without restraint, others behave in such a way because of illness. He even notes that it is the former who are more difficult to cure than those who are mentally ill or who act in an unrestrained way by habit.

Brutal traits are also mentioned by Aristotle for other types of personality. Speaking about foolish characters, he attributes the cause directly to Nature for those who are irrational and "live only through their senses in an animalistic way like some barbarians" (1149a), while others are foolish and irrational due to epilepsy or mania. On the same lines, he explains other characteristics of the personality like cowardice, debauchery, and ill-temper. There are illustrative paradigms about cowardice that he discriminates as follows: When somebody is by Nature fearful of everything, even of a mouse, he acts like animals do, while for a person afraid only of a cat the cause is an illness—an interesting differentiation and a description of what today we call "zoophobia".

Aristotle shows his conviction about the great power of Nature when he describes how man is driven to extreme conditions of brutality. Nature is responsible, he says, for the character of some malicious and perverse persons, who even the naturally unpleasant things and acts come to feel as pleasant. As examples of such depraved behaviour he mentions some savage tribes on the coast of the Black Sea, who used to lend their children to each other for various orgies and who ate raw meat, including human flesh.

Aristotle, of course, does not describe only the negative qualities given by Nature. In Book III of the *Nicomachean Ethics*, he proceeds to a long discussion of how Man can be responsible for his deeds when he has been gifted by Nature. He speaks of persons who have an acute clear-sightedness and who are in a position to judge correctly and to choose what is truly good (*agathon*). Such a person is called by the philosopher *eu-phyes*, which literally means "well-endowed-by-Nature"; in modern Greek the word means "intelligent", and I think Aristotle's definition coincides with that. People with such a gift of Nature, which is characterized in the text as the greatest and noblest, are considered privileged since they could not obtain or learn it from anyone else.

Apart from *eu-phyia* (intelligence), Aristotle accepts that Nature provides the human being with other, very significant qualities, which distinguish him from all other living creatures. The philosopher's epigrammatic phrase has remained a classic: "By far the best of animals is Man" (1253a). We have seen the importance he attributes to the natural need for coupling, originally sexual and later psychological. He extends the effect of Nature (in *Politics* he uses the words "drive of Nature" [1253a]) to Man's inclination to create a society in which to live. For that, the Stagirite believes that a human being carries since birth the potentiality of prudent and logical thinking, which helps in the development of a personality away from "unholy, wild, greedy and hedonistic tendencies" (1253a).

Aristotle's theorization is never one-sided, evident in his multifactorial approach to many subjects. In *Eudemian Ethics*, he states: "All creations (in Nature) follow the same principles, that is, the presence of all or some of the factors which exist and happen in humans" (1214a).

In accordance with such a viewpoint and in addition to the effects, direct or indirect, of Nature, the philosopher discusses other factors contributing to the development of personality and the happiness of an individual. Education is an important factor in the course of life, but, the Stagirite stresses, whatever Nature has not bestowed on someone and whatever lessons have not taught them, they should acquire by training, so as to obtain good habits (*ethos*). (Views which are extensively discussed in Chapter Ten "The effects of the environment" and Chapter Eleven "The responsibility of one's Self".)

Aristotle also believes in unexpected changes in life by chance, when unfavourable or helpful events happen. A person may find himself, abruptly, to be in a stressful situation, or, on the contrary, luck may be smiling down on him for a period. The philosopher comments on the fact that the Greek word for happiness, *eu-tychia*, is based on the word for luck, *tyche* (as also in modern Greek), thus literally meaning "good-luck".

The "comparative psychology" of Aristotle

The phrase "by far the best of animals is Man" contains in a comprehensive way the Aristotelian views on the phylogenetic and psychological relation of Man to the rest of animals. Man is basically a creature with the qualities that Nature generally provides animals, but with additional characteristics, mainly psychic, which place him on the apex of the pyramid.

The sequential way by which the ancient philosopher classifies all creatures points to his queries regarding the world, queries analogous to those that led humanity many centuries later to propose various theories—evolutionary, Darwinian, and so forth. In his book *History of Animals* Aristotle accepts a sequence (or "continuum" as he puts it [588b]) in which Nature has created the various bodies: inanimate—plants—animals—Man. He underlines the fact that some species of these big categories have small differences, so that the limits between each of them are difficult to discriminate. The series starts from the very simple and continues, gradually, to the more complex. The category of inanimate objects is followed by that of plants, which compared to the previous "seems almost animate; while in comparison to the category of animals it can be considered inanimate" (588b).

Aristotle, with his diligence about details, made an impressive number of observations on the behaviour of animals, collected information from travellers and sailors, and registered a long catalogue about the characteristics of tens of animals. He refers to the *ethos* of animals in a way that one can say he wrote one of the first "ethologies" of the animal kingdom (although, as expected, much of his data does not coincide with today's scientific evidence). Nevertheless, the descriptions he provides about the behaviour of animals and the words he uses for that, similar to those he uses for the human *ethos*—actually for the human personality—comprise in some way a "psychology" of animals which could be called "comparative", since the philosopher himself makes a direct comparison of the characterological traits of men and animals.

He says, for instance, that in most animals there are traces of psychological dispositions, although in humans they are more obvious. So many animals are meek and others unrestrained, some are courageous and others fearful, while still others are cunning and get angry easily. The Stagirite differentiates two types of characteristics in animals: those which are similar to human characteristics but differ in quantity or degree, and those which are different qualitatively, for example, men may have a tendency to art or may be wise and prudent, while animals by analogy depend on physical power or other potentialities given by Nature. I will here select out of the Aristotelian texts the characteristics of some well-known animals, wild or tamed, which suffice to illustrate the corresponding way that Aristotle compares them with human traits and the adjectives he uses, which again are the same as those for humans.

The sheep are described as easy-going and silly, because during the winter they may be lost in a wilderness if the shepherd does not send a ram to collect them, whereupon they obediently follow. The goats also are called "foolish". Horses are characterized by Aristotle as "affectionate"; he brings the paradigm of a small horse, which, if left without a mother, shall be looked after by other female horses undertaking the mother's role, even if they are barren or without milk. On the contrary, the female deer is not gifted by Nature with such motherliness; the philosopher calls her "not in the least prudent", since, as he adds, she may give birth "in the middle of a road". The *ethos* of dogs depends on their breed; those selected by shepherds are, as a rule, "brave".

Aristotle notes that Nature has given different psychic qualities to female animals than to male ones. He considers that the females are generally "softer" (608a), more easily tamed, and usually "cleverer"

(608a). In some species, the females behave in an "impertinent" way, but continue to be good mothers, while the fathers easily get "angry" with the younger ones (608b). The philosopher also mentions the information he had about elephants in India; the males are "fierce" in battle, while the females are "soulless" (610a).

In *History of Animals* Aristotle concludes that in the life of animals one observes many "imitations" (612b) of human behaviour to a greater or lesser degree. He is impressed, for instance, by the exactness in the thought of swallows when they construct their nest. He also registers intense and deep feelings of faithfulness and compassion between pigeons, which do not want to mate with a third unless they have become "a widower or a widow" (the words of the Stagirite!) and where during "the pains of labour" the male pigeon shows so much care towards and "emotional suffering" for his partner the philosopher characterizes it "astonishing".

CHAPTER TEN

The effects of the environment

Apart from the capabilities and potentialities with which Nature has supplied Man, did Aristotle accept that the environment also is influential in the shaping of the personality? The answer is definitely positive. Before I present relevant passages from his books for a more extensive discussion, I will here first make reference to a few descriptions of his indicating that even in animals the environment, animate or inanimate, has a direct effect on their behaviour and *ethos*.

During periods of shortage of food, the philosopher describes, there is war among wild animals, sometimes of the same species, until some leave the place of shortage or die. On the contrary, if there is ample food in the environment the animals live in peace; in the text there is the example of crocodiles which in ancient Egypt the priests managed to tame by caring for and feeding.

There are cases of animals and birds which show a change in their behaviour when they lose their partner and remain alone in their environment. The Stagirite cites the case of a cock that, when the mother of his young chickens dies, starts "taking them around and feeding them" (631b). The surprising change mentioned surpasses a simple alteration in behaviour, since such a cock no more acts as a male: he does not crow at dawn nor does he want to have sex with a new hen. A similar change of gender role and instinctual drives takes place, according to *History of Animals*, in the case of a hen that fights and beats a cock; such a hen then begins to crow early in the morning and even tries to have sex with other hens!

The argument by the ancient philosopher continues as follows: "All animals act according to their feelings and then the actions of their behaviour determine their final *ethos* ('personality')" (631b). He even proceeds further with what we today would call a psychobiological comment: Not only *ethos* can change, but also some parts of the body under certain conditions in the environment. As an example he mentions a hen, who, when alone and victorious, not only adopts the opposite gender's role, but also shows relevant change in its tail, cockscomb, and so forth.

Aristotle discusses in addition the effect of the human environment on animals and how their behaviour and characterological qualities can be altered. He specifically states that some animals can be taught by and can learn from Man, mainly those which not only just see images and hear noises, but can understand the meaning of what they see and hear. A striking example is that of the wild elephants that can be tamed. Some were in ancient times guided to be brave in the war, while others were trained to be peaceful and to help in heavy jobs. There is a detailed description in the text about how the tamer hunts the elephant, jumps on it, forces the animal to be obedient, and at the end they both collaborate in order to throw down trees, walls, and so forth.

The child and its first environment

In order to better understand the way that Aristotle accepts the channels through which the environment affects the formation of the personality, it is necessary to examine first the psychic qualities that he considers as existing in Man at his birth and during the first years of life. On what substratum will the outer environment act and in what way will the effect take place?

We have already seen the philosopher's opinion that Nature endows the human being with many fundamental qualities, some of which are also found in animals, in addition to psychological traits that place him at the apex of the "continuum" in Nature's creations.

Nevertheless, many of the latter characteristics only become evident with the passing of years and in the age of maturity.

What capabilities then are at the disposal of a human baby or small child? A very eloquent answer is contained in a passage of *History of Animals*. "During childhood," the philosopher remarks, "one can see traces of characteristics to be found in the personality of later years, but it can be said that during the first period the soul of a child does not differ much from the 'soul' of a wild animal" (588a). The comparison made here between children and animals follows the viewpoint of the Stagirite we met before through which he approaches the existence of Man as originally biological (or one can say "animalistic").

The biological aspect of the human organism is even better clarified in other books of Aristotle, where it is clearly stated that the first functions of a baby, in addition to the nutritive and sense-perception, are instinctual—and more so appetitive. In *Politics*, there is an important position about the fact that desires and appetites are present in the child since the day of its birth, while logical thinking is programmed by Nature to develop with the passing of years. In Book III of the *Nicomachean Ethics*, it is pointed out that children live by following their desires and that appetites, with pleasure as their objective, exist in them to a great degree.

"Appetites", as we had the chance of discussing in a previous chapter (Chapter Four "Volition [will] and psychomotor function"), correspond in the Aristotelian philosophy to the instinctual drives of the psychoanalytic theory. They constitute a psychobiological function that originates from internal tendencies and impulsive dispositions for immediate satisfaction, whereupon "desires" are produced, unrestrained against any logic. Aristotle describes the qualities of appetites in many of his books. In *On the Soul*, in a laconic and comprehensive way, he states: "Appetites activate one against any logical thinking" (433a). The need for the satisfaction of appetites through bodily actions is expressed in *Rhetoric*, where once again it is stressed that they are illogical (*a-logoi*) in that they do not follow any prudent thinking, and in addition examples are given of bodily demands directed by Nature: thirst, hunger, touch, smells, sounds, and (in the years of maturity) sexual intercourse. The senses, therefore, and the instinctual needs are those being satisfied by the actions of appetites. The impulsive tendencies for immediate satisfaction and the insatiable nature of the appetites are clearly pointed out by the philosopher in Book III of *Nicomachean Ethics*, where he says that "their desire for pleasure is so greedy, that even during gratification their innate drive increases" (1119b).

Aristotle's opinion that the child since its birth is flooded by appetites, innate intense and insatiable tendencies, is important for our discussion here regarding the relation of the child to its first environment. The latter is obliged to curtail the child's demands, mostly somatic and illogical, and the philosopher refers to those having that duty: the parents, teachers, and lawgivers. The child must become obedient through the teachings of the tutors, like the adults whose desires must be directed by logic; this view in the Aristotelian texts (together with those previously discussed) indicates that the human being in childhood is primarily considered as having biological-animalistic qualities, as well as traces of more mature traits (like judgement and logic), which, however, need time to develop.

The human environment (family, educators, and fellow-citizens) is the determining factor influencing the course of the child towards maturity—a subject that will be discussed more extensively in the following pages. A particular method in such a process of breeding and educating a child, which Aristotle repeatedly mentions, are the instructions given to the child so that it becomes accustomed-by-habit (*ethos*) to act in the right way and with virtue—and not succumb to appetites (see more in Chapter Eleven "The responsibility of one's Self").

Parental care

Aristotle, expressing the view that for the formation of a mature personality a good physical state is a prerequisite since the first days of one's life, proceeds to examine the best possible conditions even before one's birth. So he discusses subjects like the more appropriate time for marriage of the parents, the best time to give birth to a child, the physical and mental health of a pregnant woman, and so on. The discussion is written in *Politics*, a book which deals with the ancient Greek states and their laws, where the philosopher suggests that certain of the above subjects should be guided by relevant legislation.

The Stagirite, taking as an upper limit for the ability of procreation the age of 70 for men and, for women, 50 years, considers that the best age for a woman to have a child is around 18 years and for a man below 37, "when the bodies are in their prime" (1335a). He also mentions many other details (many of which may not be medically correct today), but what interests us here are some psychological comments of his regarding the child and the age of its parents: If the difference in age is very great, the aged parents will not have enough chances of enjoying their children's gratitude, nor will they be in a position to help them in a satisfactory way; on the other hand, if the difference is very small there will be psychological difficulties in their relations, since the children will not respect them, seeing it as if they were of the same age.

For the period of pregnancy, Aristotle gives advice on physical, as well as psychological, subjects. He urges pregnant women to not stay indolent but rather to be on the move, and to eat nutritive food. He also advises that they should remain calm and for that they should go on certain days and pray in temples of Gods who protect those "having the honour of creating" (1335b). (Very rarely the philosopher proceeds to such a proposal, which, I take it, is not done in a theocratic but rather in a "psychotherapeutic" spirit.)

The Stagirite in *Politics*, commenting that the newborn should enjoy all the good things that a mother can give ("like a plant from its mother-earth" [1335b]), makes some observations of his own and deals with more practical themes relevant to medicine and paedagogics. He underlines the nutritive value of milk, and advises that the mother should not consume wine. The babies should be allowed to move their limbs freely, so that they are not abnormally twisted, as it seems was "the habit by some nations using mechanical instruments" (1336a)!

Aristotle considers right that children should get used to hardships from their early days and brings the example of the Celts, "the barbarians who dipped into a cold river" (1336b) even the babies. The important aspect of such a view is that the philosopher believes that the above tactics on behalf of the parents not only improve physical health, but also contribute to the shaping of a more enduring and strong character. The view is in accordance with the Stagirite's general opinion that he steadily and clearly expresses: For any trait of the personality that can be acquired by the children through habit (*ethos*), it is better if they are instructed from their first years and the process should continue in the same way step-by-step.

For children up to 5 years of age, Aristotle advises that the parents must not scold them if they cry; rather, they should help them get involved in games and gymnastics, so that they do not become lazy. Playing should not be too hard and tiring, nor sluggish. More helpful games are those imitating future activities or professions, thus contributing to the formation of a more creative personality in the growing child.

Myths and tales are also regarded as very important at this age. The ethical side of one's developing personality will be influenced if one lives in an environment with filthy talk; he will start adopting such language and at the end will proceed to obscene actions, says Aristotle. The philosopher makes a psychological remark: Whatever one experiences at a very young age, one keeps in his soul as more dear—that is why a child should be brought up in an environment without malice or enmities. The nurturing of a child until the age of 7 years should take place at home, since the interactions with the parents during those years are very significant; the child is thus protected from outside bad influences.

In *Politics*, reference is made to what lawgivers should do on such subjects so that the family is helped. Vulgar language in public places should be prohibited by law, as well as anything provocative that would have an adverse effect on the personality of youngsters. The same holds true for theatrical performances, paintings, or statues which imitate indecent behaviour. The philosopher is of the opinion that adolescents should not be allowed to certain festivities where adults get drunk, and so forth, until they come of age; "by that time", he contends, "education will have made them invulnerable" (1336b).

For Aristotle, the love and care of the parents for their children exist always beyond any doubt. The father is presented putting the rules for the bringing up of the children and giving the basic lines for the formation of their personality, without rejecting any one of them. The father is compared in a parallel way as similar to a good king taking care of his subjects, and in contrast to the Persians who behaved tyrannically towards their children as if towards slaves. The importance and magnitude of fatherly love is stressed, and explained as originating from the fact that the father has actually been "the cause of the children's existence, their greatest good" (1161a), apart from his care for maintaining and educating them. Mention is also made to an analogous bestowing of benefits by one's ancestors.

Motherly love is even greater than that of fathers; it is absolute and can be taken as the model for any ideal love. As proof of this, Aristotle brings the example of mothers who for various reasons have given their child to be brought up by others and yet they love the child without asking for anything in return; they are satisfied when they see it prosper, even though the child does not recognize them as their real mother: "That happens because real love consists in giving than in receiving affection" (1159a). Furthermore, whatever one achieves with great effort, one loves more, and therefore mothers provide greater affection for their children (*philo-teknoterai*) because of the tiring labour and birth they had, and since they consider the children as belonging more to them, as their own creations. The devotion of a mother to her children is by far above the degree of any other type of love, since "she always participates in their joys and their sorrows" (1166a).

The above observations by Aristotle in *Nicomachean Ethics* indicate clearly the importance he attributes to the emotional support and security the parents offer to their children, elements more than necessary (as we today know) for a solid and healthy development of one's personality. The influence of the parental environment is also affected by education, which is the responsibility mainly of the father. The more time a child lives and communicates with its parents, the more this relation will bring benefits to the child's character—benefits useful and pleasant.

The way that Aristotle deals with parental care, attributing its origin to a drive of Nature, can be considered on the one hand a biological (in today's terms) approach, but at the same time one which has definite psychological parameters. Let us listen to the philosopher's own words: "Parents love their children as if being a part of themselves, and the children love their parents because they have originated from them ... Parents love their children the way they love themselves, because whatever was created by them is a kind of other self existing separately (in another form)" (1161b). From the phraseology, it becomes evident that in spite of the biological basis of birth, there develops an emotional identification between parents and children, one which cannot but affect the personality structure of the latter.

The significant influence of the family environment is clearly expressed by Aristotle in his discussion about the relations between brothers. He attributes a similarity of characterological traits seen in brothers to the same way of rearing by the (same) parents—"the more they have been trained in a similar way, the more they are alike in character (*homo-etheis*)" (1162a). He also gives emphasis to the time factor: brothers who are closer in age or have lived together at home for longer periods develop a familiarity among themselves, a familiarity that impacts on their emotional reactions to each other.

Effects of education

Aristotle examines the effects of education in Book VIII of *Politics* in the context of his concern about the best conditions under which Man's personality can be formed, so that there will be excellent citizens. Among the questions he puts is, first and foremost: What education should be given—which will be its targets and by what methods? The philosopher refers to the different opinions that existed in his era: "One should be taught only the useful in life or those guiding to virtue?" (1337a) Is the development of intellect preferable or should education aim to the shaping of a moral character (*psyches ethos*)? (It seems there was then a similar problem like today's dilemma between practical, technological knowledge and a general education towards higher moral and aesthetic standards.)

Aristotle presents another difficulty in planning a good educational system: Even those in favour of promoting the moral and cultural aspects of the personality through education would not agree on what is a virtue—the notion and content of virtue. Consequently, they could not agree on the programme of teaching.

Aristotle's conviction that education is a basic means for the development of good characteristics in a personality is shown in many of his texts. Education and virtue go hand in hand, he says, and co-operate fully for Man's happiness. He brings many paradigms to corroborate his claim; for instance, that education keeps away bad features of a character, such as greed for money or extreme ambitions. In another passage he repeats his opinion that important personalities are produced by three factors—"Nature, habituation and logic"—adding, nevertheless, "the rest is the job of education" (1332a). The philosopher, however, is a realist and accepts that some persons are by Nature inadequate and that it may be impossible for education to make them important.

The Stagirite gives particular significance to the motive that leads one to education. If a person wants to learn for his own satisfaction, or for the sake of his friends, or in order to acquire virtue, then education is of value. However, if somebody is led to education in order to obey others or for money, then it is a mean and servile action.

Having a practical approach, and not only theoretical, for many aspects of human activities the philosopher does not exclude instruction for "those of the useful things which are necessary in life" (1337b). He even extends his advice to the time available for leisure, by saying that from childhood one should be taught to work for the sake of leisure, that is, to engage in work in such a way so as to enjoy during leisure higher, intellectual pleasures.

* * *

The educational programme that Aristotle proposes consists of four courses of lessons: "letters", drawing, gymnastics, and music.

By "letters", it is meant reading and writing, mathematics, and sometimes literature or history. The philosopher writes very little in *Politics* about this course, in contrast to the other three, most probably thinking that it is of less importance in the shaping of personality. He mentions that "letters" are useful in life as they give somebody the opportunity to acquire further knowledge, as well as helping him to handle his household and political affairs.

Drawing, according to the Stagirite, enriches the personality as it provides young people with an observant eye for beauty and makes them better equipped to judge articles of art.

Gymnastics is a practical course necessary for building a strong and healthy body, features that are considered by Aristotle to be a prerequisite for a smooth and sound development of the mind and soul. That is why he urges parents to first put their children in the hands of physical instructors. Body training promotes the virtue of courage, and with that a person acquires initiative and acts bravely.

He learns to struggle with patience and persistence, and when the training takes place in front of old rulers a youngster gets accustomed to showing respect. So in fact, the course of gymnastics, the philosopher remarks, contributes to obtaining the sense of the mean—the middle way that one should apply generally in life.

Aristotle opposes hard exercise stating that an athlete's training is not suitable for everybody. He criticizes the Spartians for making their youth ferocious instead of noble, since one-sided, bodily toughness in education hampers mental work. A contrary effect is produced by play, which provides relief from exertion and relaxation in the mind.

It is noteworthy that the ancient philosopher suggests that physical training is necessary not only for men but also for women.

Aristotle devotes a great part of the last book of *Politics* to music. To the question of whether music can contribute to the moulding of one's personality, his answer is positive, and in order to support his claim he brings several arguments: "When we listen to some pieces of music our mood changes; the Olympian melodies (those connected with the Gods) make our soul enthusiastic" (1340a). One is differently affected according to the harmonies of the compositions he listens to; some produce a sadder and graver temperament, others a moderate one, while soft music brings relaxation of the mind.

A similar effect is produced by the rhythms, since some are quick and lively; others are slower and emotion-provoking. So rhythms and melodies may produce a feeling of calmness, or of courage, or even of anger. These emotional states, Aristotle believes, have a more lasting effect on the personality, especially during the tender years of youth, in contrast to the influence of other pieces of art (statues, paintings) which is very slight and only temporary.

The philosopher reminds us of the power which music possesses in education, when he recommends that children should listen to "good melodies with good rhythm" (1341b). In contrast, he refers to those who prefer to listen to "over-coloured, noisy, vulgar" music, people he calls "deviant souls".

It is medically interesting that Aristotle mentions "people who are affected by religious hymns, to a point that they get inspired and excited, and then become calm as if therapeutically treated (*iatreia*)" (1342a). This "psychotherapeutic" release of emotions the philosopher names *katharsis*, like the process in ancient tragedies. He also adds that such an effect is more obvious in very sensitive, pitiful, or phobic persons, as well as in passive personalities.

In addition to music as a beneficial part of education, the Stagirite accepts its role as amusement and pleasure. That is one of the reasons he advises that children should be taught to play an instrument. Other reasons are for them to acquire better aesthetic criteria and to appreciate good compositions and their performance.

CHAPTER ELEVEN

The responsibility of one's Self

The qualities with which Nature supplies Man, somatic and psychic, and the various effects which he receives from the environment, after a period produce for him the possibility to contribute himself to the course of his life that follows. How much this is done consciously or unconsciously, to what degree this is the result of the laws of learning, and so forth, is a matter of theorization, according to the "school" (psychoanalytic, behavioural, or other) to which each researcher belongs. In any way, Man goes through a developmental process, during which at various stages his own Self more and more takes over his fortune undergoing certain intrapsychic procedures. (The word "Self" is used in this chapter in its everyday meaning, and not in the sense it holds in the writings of the psychoanalyst Kohut or elsewhere where it is used as a specific term.)

In this chapter, there will be a discussion of the views of Aristotle on the above subject in relevance to the formation of the personality, and an attempt to find possible corresponding, parallel, or opposing theories to those of modern psychology and psychiatry.

Most "schools" of psychology today accept, perhaps with different terminology, the existence of a conscious and a non-conscious Self. Let us see in short what psychoanalysis has to teach on the subject. Freud spoke about the Unconscious, the Conscious, and the Preconscious. The Unconscious contains those psychic experiences and processes which for reasons of homeostasis and equilibrium are kept away from the conscious perception. In the Conscious state Man is in an alert condition, has full knowledge of himself and the environment and can handle outside stimuli, as well as his personal needs. In contrast, the Unconscious escapes perception because its contents include unacceptable and prohibited desires which can become evident only indirectly in dreams, accidental mistakes (*lapsus linguae*), contradictory actions, in certain psychotic ideas, hallucinations, and so forth. In the Preconscious, there are processes and experiences which can become conscious more easily.

Later Freud developed his structural theory of personality distinguishing three parts: the Ego, the Superego, and the Id. The Id is considered the part that contains the instinctual drives and is found at an unconscious level. It is essentially the motivating energy for every function, biological originally (nutrition, aggression, reproduction) with psychological manifestations that follow (erotic love, motherhood, etc).

The Ego is that part which acts as an intermediate between inner drives and various prohibitions; being mostly at the conscious level, it keeps contact with reality and shapes the relations of a person with the outer world.

The Superego is considered the part that determines the moral behaviour and the ideals that the Ego is searching to accomplish. It therefore helps the Ego in controlling the instinctual drives. The Superego originates from parental (mainly paternal) figures and values in childhood, when the rule of reward-or-punishment is strong.

It is understood that the Ego has a synthetic role trying to harmonize the impulsive and persistent instinctual demands of the Id with the commands of the Superego through mechanisms of defence, so that without leaving the basic needs the moral values are not violated. A mature Ego facilitates the social adaptation based on good judgement and logic, acting with flexibility and responsibility and postponing or changing a demand for satisfaction whenever needed.

The structure of the personality according to Aristotle

Let us now see how Aristotle deals with and analyses the subject of the structure of the personality—"the particles (*moria*, parts) of the soul" (1102a), to use his terminology. He distinguishes two parts of the soul, the irrational and the rational, and, with clarity, he states that the first is not based on logic (*a-logon*), while the other functions according to the laws of logic (*logos*). His further analysis gives details that remind one of some positions of modern psychology.

The Stagirite divides the *irrational* part into two again: the vegetative and the appetitive, full of desires.

The *vegetative* is common to animals and plants, and constitutes the motivating force for their nourishment and increase. Aristotle elucidates that it exists in the embryonic period, as well as in the fully developed organism. Essentially, therefore, it is composed of innate functions (rather than elements of the personality), the nutritive and reproductive, that is, biological (as we would today say), the former for survival of the individual and the latter for the continuation of the species. In psychoanalytic terms, one may say that the first corresponds to the aggressive and the other to the sexual instincts. The philosopher repeats at many points in the *Nicomachean Ethics* that "the vegetative part has no relation at all with logic" (1102b).

The *appetitive-desiring* particle of the soul is also all the time opposing logic, but under certain circumstances it succumbs to the latter's principles (see Chapter Three "Thought and judgement" and Chapter Four "Volition [will] and psychomotor function"). It exists by Nature, Aristotle says, as a part of one's being, fighting and defying the reasonable part. Yet, he adds, it is doing that without any skill, clumsily (*a-technos*) (1102b), so that it does not give a psychologically healthy solution (see more on this well-aimed observation in the Section "Intrapsychic conflicts" in Chapter Eleven). We have seen in Chapter Four "Volition (will) and psychomotor function" that desires are closely connected with appetites, which in the Aristotelian texts correspond in a great degree to the unconscious instinctual drives of psychoanalysis. There is a very comprehensive line showing the impulsive nature of the desires at an unconscious level: "The desiring drives of morally incontinent people take always an opposite stand (against logic)" (1102b). It clearly denotes the unrestrained force of the desires that drag people away, so that (almost unwillingly) they behave contrary to common sense.

There is another equally interesting paragraph in *Nicomachean Ethics* regarding the whole *alogon* particle of the soul, which points even more strongly to the unconscious nature of this irrational part: "It is more active during sleep", Aristotle informs, "and to the same extent in both good and bad personalities" (1102b). He even mentions that it motivates certain processes that affect the appearance of dreams. In view of the above remarks, which show the philosopher's sharp insight into the intrapsychic phenomena, one cannot avoid a parallelism between the irrational element in the Aristotelian philosophy and the analogous part in the psychoanalytic theory, the Id, which provides the unconscious material for the dreams.

The *rational* part of the soul forces the irrational to show discipline and follow its orders depending on the personality of the individual. That, for instance, happens in the case of a morally strong person, the Stagirite tells us. His next paradigm demonstrates even more the conscious and practical ability of this part to act: In prudent and brave men, the irrational particle is much more obedient to the principles of reason. The basic features, then, of the rational part of the soul seem very close to those of the modern notion of conscious Ego.

Of very great interest is the subdivision that Aristotle feels necessary to make regarding the rational element. He distinguishes the "mainly and strictly logical" (1103a) which acts by itself, following its own principles (like in the examples just above), and a second one that he does not name with a term but describes in a periphrastic way: "a part which exists as if listening to the father's commands" (1103a). Reference to the influence of fatherly views (and consequently their intrapsychic incorporation) is made in the same chapter of the *Nicomachean Ethics*, where the philosopher writes that the appetitive desires obey the rational part "like when we say that somebody follows the logic of his father, and not like when he accepts the logic of mathematics" (1102b). The distinction of a whole "particle of the soul" having as its content only the father's commands cannot be accidental. Most probably the deep psychological insight of Aristotle led him to that statement, which essentially is very near the nucleus of what centuries later was formulated by psychoanalysis and is known as the Superego. Indeed the compari son of the impersonal mathematical logic followed by the "main and strict logic" with the one just mentioned as resulting from an interpersonal emotional connection with the father points to the same conclusion.

Intrapsychic conflicts

A psychological equilibrium is the target towards which the mental functions of every person continuously aim, a homeostasis, so that they are effective in life. Irrespective of the theory one follows regarding the structure of the personality, everyone accepts that its parts should act in harmony in order for a smooth course to be achieved. Yet homeostasis is not usually present after an easy and painless process; many obstacles, both from outside and from the inner self, intervene and lead to various conflicts.

In psychoanalytic terms, the conflicts happen between the Ego, the Id, and the Superego. The Ego as the basic representative of the conscious self, tries all the time to keep a balance in the relations of an individual with his surroundings. Nature, on the other hand, has its own targets: perpetuation of life through the survival of the species—of Man. For that reason, the human being is driven by biologically determined instinctual tendencies towards self-preservation and procreation of offspring. These instinctual drives belonging to the Id in their struggle for satisfaction are confronted with many prohibitions, from the outside world but also from the inside, the moral code of each person, the Superego, which originates from parental values during childhood. For the conflicts that follow between Id and Superego it is the duty of the Ego to undertake and settle the differences by using various mechanisms of defence (repression, sublimation, etc.), but in case these fail the individual develops anxiety and other symptoms.

Let us see now in what way Aristotle approaches the subject. First of all, beyond any doubt the philosopher accepts the existence of a significant intrapsychic conflict between two main mental functions, when he repeats in various texts that "Reason (*logos*) and desires run contrary to each other" (433b). Reason belongs to the mental function of thought and desires to volition. The forceful fight implied to be happening during the conflict is demonstrated by the features with which the Stagirite characterizes the desires. We had the chance of discussing them at various points (Chapters Three, Four, and Ten): "The desires are in the sphere of the irrational" (432b) and "they have an incessant appetite for hedonistic pleasure" (414b). Desires push a man to demand immediate satisfaction, without any postponement, because they make him think that only the present is pleasurable and forget all about the future. In addition, a biological, instinctual quality is attributed by the philosopher to the appetitive desires, as is evident in his statement in *On the Soul* that they constitute the force activating and directing an animal to move towards a pleasant object.

All the above characteristics (which coincide largely with those of the psychoanalytic instinctual drives of the Id) provide the impulsive energy (*energeia* is literally written in that passage) for opposition against *logos* (which, as we have a little before discussed, is very similar to a part of the conscious Ego). *Logos* then, rational thinking, has the difficult task to confront and control the greediness of the appetitive desires. The fight is even more difficult in younger people. We have been told in *Politics* that logic develops with the passing of years and that the children since birth are carried away by their instinctual desires, searching all the time for pleasures. When a person is mature enough, he activates the function of wish (*voulesis*; see Chapter Four), according to Aristotle, which can oppose desires and appetites, so that the person can live within reasonable limits. The philosopher's comment on wish *vs.* desire is clear and laconic: "Wish functions within logic, while desire remains in the irrational" (432b).

A direct reference of intrapsychic conflicts is made in several works of Aristotle. In *On the Soul* he describes how "wish by forming rational opinions after deliberate (and therefore conscious) thinking can beat desires" (434a), while at other times if the appetitive desires are intense these may put aside reasoning. This conflict is repeated in *Nicomachean Ethics* where, it is stated, "there is a particle in the soul which reacts against the rational element" (1102b). Even when the outcome of the conflict is victorious for the desires, the result is not necessarily a normal one, since the process is done as a rule "clumsily" (*a-technos*, "without art" literally [1102b]). Such a case for the soul is similar to what happens in paralyzed limbs of the body, he says, when one cannot command them anymore. The comparison is most aptly done, since today we know that if the Id is not fully gratified, or the Ego is not able to fully repress the instinctual desires (using "artless" defences), then the resulting condition may be psychologically "paralytic", with many symptoms.

The difference of scope for the two antagonizing sides is clarified in another passage: Thought calls us to hold back for the sake of the future, while desire drives us to get satisfaction in the present. So once again, the importance of personality is stressed: Temperate people restrain themselves and follow reason, even when they have an appetite for a desirable object. In contrast, morally weak people act in accordance with desires.

Freedom of choice and decision

Apart from the parallel way of thinking or even the similarities that a researcher may find to exist between the views of Aristotle about the structure of the personality and those of modern psychology, there are also basic differences. The most significant is the importance that the philosopher gives to the possibilities of a person to improve his own Self in comparison to what some modern "schools" today teach. For instance, psychoanalytic theory, although accepting an essential contribution of the conscious Ego to the shaping of the personality, nevertheless considers of greater importance the continuous struggle of the instinctual drives and the prohibitions at an unconscious level. Such a conflict is accepted, as we have seen, by the Stagirite too, but he leaves the final outcome to a steering by the conscious Self, to which he attributes several qualities that make Man more efficient: choice (*proairesis*), deliberation (*vouleusis*), *ethos*, and others. The philosopher presents these potentialities of the human character from his own philosophical standpoint, that is, the accomplishment of virtue and happiness, but here we must discuss the subject in relevance to the formation of the personality.

To choice, Aristotle devotes a whole chapter in *Nicomachean Ethics* and examines its particular features, showing his great analytic ability concerning the mental processes and their different variations. He distinguishes choice from wish, opinion, and others, while the most important comparison he makes is with desire. In contrast to desire, there exists no choice in irrational beings like animals, which of course have instinctual drives. While desire is related to pleasure and in case of frustration to a painful condition, choice has no such connections. In three words this antithesis is phrased by the philosopher: "Desire opposes choice" (1111b). He also brings a typical example to indicate the characterological difference which the one or the other element attributes to an individual's personality: A man is unrestrained when he acts according to his desires and not by choice, while the one who acts on the basis of choice and is not influenced by desire is a self-restrained and morally strong man.

From such comparisons, one concludes that choice follows logical rules, opposes instinctual desires, and is practiced by self-disciplined people. The definition of choice is put by Aristotle in an interrogative way: "Is choice perhaps the result of a thought which had been previously carried out?" (1112a). And the answer is positive in the text: Yes, since choice presupposes reasoning and generally an intellectual process beforehand. Its name indicates that, the philosopher himself remarks: *Pro-airesis* is a compound word and means choosing and pre-ferring something prior to any other.

Freedom of choice and preference is a quality which a mature man can handle and which, as Aristotle underlines, children and animals do not possess. He even considers it a trait from which one can judge an individual's personality, more so than the latter's actions. His line "Our character can be determined from whether we make good or bad choices" (1112a), shows the importance that the Stagirite gives to the responsibility of one's Self in life—as we will discuss in the following pages more extensively.

At this point, the reader may wonder: What is the difference between choice and wish (*voulesis*), since we have been told earlier that wish also follows logic, consciously opposes desires, and reaches conclusions after serious thinking? Aristotle foresees the question and, accepting that wish is a very close phenomenon, proceeds to a detailed clarification. First, wish can have a wider spectrum of objects and may aim at impossible targets (for example, a wish for immortality), while *pro-airesis* does not choose objects beyond those attainable. Second, wish is more related to the final aim, while choice is involved with the means by which the target will be achieved. A classical example is given in the text: We all wish to be healthy, but our choice concerns the means by which we will remain healthy. The distinction is clear: Choice extends to those that are within our power.

Another quality that Aristotle registers as belonging exclusively to human mental abilities is deliberation (*vouleusis*). It is an intellectual process, the special characteristics and the role of which the ancient philosopher analyses in *Nicomachean Ethics* (Chapter three of Book III). Basically, it is a function of internal, detailed and step-by-step thinking with one's Self, a syllogism during which all data about a subject are presented to the Self. Out of these, the individual has the freedom to choose, select, and, at the end, decide. So deliberation precedes choice. Otherwise, the two have a close relation shown by their common features. They both are after what is feasible and realistic, and they are both looking for the means that can lead to the ultimate goal. We think and study those that are within our power, the Stagirite says, and we do not doubt our intentions—like the doctors who do not deliberate whether they should or should not cure a patient, but only how best they can do it. So by deliberation and choice one is freely seeking for the relevant tools and how to use them.

Emphasis is given by Aristotle on the freedom of thought and choice available for Man in a passage where he states that in case there are many ways by which something can be attained, Man has the possibility to search for the one which is the best and easiest. In spite of the philosopher's position according to which the responsibility for a final decision rests with the conscious Self of a person, he is realistic enough not to disregard the probably restricted capabilities of certain individuals; so he advises that for serious problems, when one does not feel sufficiently equipped to examine ("to diagnose" is the verb in the text, [1112b]) all parameters, one is excused to ask from others their views. And he justifies that by commenting that whatever has been done with the help of friends, has in a way been accomplished by us, since the original move was ours.

When the Self undertakes responsibility

The freedom of choice and decision, which the ancient philosopher registers, allows one to entrust the initiative to one's Self, and especially to "the dominant and ruling part of the Self, which can make the final choice" (1113a). By that phrase, it is clear that Aristotle imparts the main responsibility for one's decision to the thinking processes of the conscious Self, the actions of which characterize also one's personality. Furthermore, in a long discussion of the subject in Chapter Five, Book III of *Nicomachean Ethics*, the Stagirite considers that for a mature person such actions decided by the conscious Self are in fact voluntary, and therefore the responsibility belongs to that particular Self.

The theorization, of course, in a book of ethics is mostly done from moral, legal, and generally philosophical aspects, but there are also some points with psychological interest, which it is worthwhile to discuss. Aristotle's argumentation goes like this: It depends on our Self to do something or not to do it; it is up to us to say yes or say no. Therefore our Self is responsible for our actions whether good or bad. His conclusion is that it is in our power to be virtuous or wicked when the initiative is left to us.

The philosopher ascribes responsibility also to persons who out of ignorance proceed to punishable offences. Ignorance is not excused, he believes, when one offends in a state of drunkenness which he could avoid, or when one neglects to examine what is proper or not, or if one is careless enough and lives in a loose and self-indulgent manner. The Stagirite considers responsible even sick people, in case their illness has been the result of not conforming to the guidelines of their doctor, or because they became physically handicapped through lack of exercise, although the initiative was at their disposal. He exempts individuals with other conditions, for example, the blind by nature or due to accident for which they are not to blame.

It is evident that the viewpoint from which Aristotle approaches the subject is basically that of imputing or not responsibility to an adult for his actions, the way it happens today for some legal cases in Forensic Psychiatry. Intrapsychic conflicts or other mental processes which probably may have contributed for somebody to be led to drunkenness, negligence, carelessness, wickedness, etc. (factors which would be investigated by a modern school of "deep psychology") are not taken into consideration in this text, although the Stagirite had diagnosed the role of such psychic phenomena elsewhere, as we have seen.

Aristotle, most probably having in mind the multifactorial way of formation of the character, distinguishes the responsibility of an individual for his actions from that for the habitual characteristics (*hexis*) of his personality. Our actions and our characteristics, he says, are not in the same way voluntary, because we are masters of our actions from the beginning to the end, being conscious of all the facts and phases, while for the characteristics of our personality we can control only what happens at the beginning without perceiving the development of later stages (during which other factors are added). The Stagirite was convinced, therefore, that there are possibilities of conscious contribution to the developmental course of the personality by one's own Self, but only during the first stages. His words are: "For the qualities of our character we are in some way jointly responsible" ("accomplices" is the actual word he uses!) (1114b). So the contribution of the Self is only partial, since it is accepted that other unknown to us factors are added—meaning obviously the influence of Nature, of the environment, and of the intrapsychic processes—factors which the ancient philosopher wisely investigated and which we had the chance of discussing in previous chapters (see Chapters Nine and Ten).

The Aristotelian "ethos" and "hexis"

In many treatises of Aristotle, there is often reference to "*ethos*" and "*hexis*" with description of their properties, showing the importance that the philosopher gave to those two concepts for the psychic development of Man (and his course towards virtue and happiness—the philosopher's main interest). Here relevant passages will be discussed from four big works: *Nicomachean Ethics, Politics, Eudemian Ethics*, and *Rhetoric*.

The significance the Stagirite attributes to the role of *ethos* for the psychobiological course of Man is shown by the fact that he registers *ethos* on an equal basis with Nature and logic—two main factors of that course. In *Politics* he writes that good and illustrious people result out of three factors—Nature, *ethos*, and logic—since on these their character depends. In *Nicomachean Ethics*, he adds that it is commonly accepted that some lucky men become virtuous by Nature, others by *ethos*, while logic and teaching are not effective in all cases. Aristotle compares the role of the three factors in Man with what happens in other creatures; he notes that in animals the rules of Nature are dominant and to a smaller degree *ethos* (in the sense of habitual acting), while only Man has logic at his disposal and, through reasoning, may be persuaded to act against the commands of Nature or previous habits.

What then is the meaning of the term *ethos* in Aristotelian philosophy? We have already met a satisfactory explanation when we were discussing Man's potentialities (see Chapter Nine "The gifts of Nature"): "Virtues do not develop in us by Nature, nor contrary to Nature; rather we are equipped by Nature to receive them and then they are completed by habit (*ethos*); first we have the functional potentialities endowed by Nature and then we act accordingly" (1103a). Among the examples Aristotle gives is that one cannot become a guitar player if he does not actually play and get exercise with a guitar. So *ethos* is a process: by repeated actions and exercise one is habituated to certain types of behaviour. The experience obtained during such activities and the way that one is accustomed by habit lead to the shaping of certain characteristics of the personality: *hexis*. The philosopher is clear about it: "*Hexis* is the end result of repeated, habitual actions" (1114a).

The Stagirite, in order to support his view that exercise is necessary for certain of our characteristics, presents many examples: If everyone of us were by birth good or bad, then we would not need teachers. We become just or unjust according to the interactions we have had with our fellowmen. Only by passing through misfortunes, we become accustomed to either courage or fear and thus become brave or coward-like. In a similar way men can learn, according to the philosopher, to restrain their instinctual desires and so behave prudently and calmly, while if not they become promiscuous and angry. In *Eudemian Ethics*, we read that if one lives in a wicked environment, one by habituation is driven to wicked and punishable actions. In *Rhetoric*, the philosopher insists: "If one has been doing something many times, then his actions continue by habit (*ethos*)" (1369b).

Aristotle by his syllogism again attributes responsibility to one's Self: One has the freedom to choose, his decisions determine the actions he will take, and (starting from these initial stages) if one repeatedly acts in the same way, then by habit he acquires certain (more permanent) personality characteristics (*hexis*). The outcome of this whole procedure may be positive or negative; the philosopher states that *hexis* is the characteristic attitude we keep towards our passions, for example, our attitude to anger is bad if we get angry vehemently or weakly, but if moderately our *hexis* is good. It is evident that Aristotle's theorization comes from a moral and paedagogical viewpoint, but if one sees it in a psychological frame it can be said to be very close to the behavioural rules of learning theory.

The great strength of several types of *hexis*, although acquired characteristics, is underlined by the Stagirite in the comparison he makes with the strength of Nature. It is very hard, he says, to change the learned habits because they resemble the traits bestowed by Nature—so in fact he considers *hexis* a "second Nature". The only difference lies in the fact that Nature has given innate personality characteristics since birth, while *ethos* and consequently *hexis* come after long and repeated actions. Once the conscious Self shows its will to consistently apply such actions, the person will gradually obtain much more strength and effectiveness; for example, one will be able more easily to refrain from pleasures, or with greater courage, one will face dangers, if he despises each one of them from the very beginning.

The above are in harmony with Aristotle's position that experience obtained by habit should start very early in life. "It is a practice of no small importance for the child's development", he advises; "it is of very great importance, it is rather of absolute (*pan*) need" (1103b). He deposits that duty first to the parents and later to the teachers. To the question whether such learning based on habit should precede teaching based on logic, the philosopher answers positively, since, as he has presented elsewhere, reasoning prevails in children much later.

Aristotle, recognizing that there are obstacles in the training of youngsters for virtue, since they are full of desires and difficult to be disciplined, proceeds to the following argumentation: If in the personality of an individual there is beforehand something producing an inclination towards virtue, something which wishes only the good actions and prevents the bad ones, then everything runs smoothly. If not, then there must be laws and regulations on how to nurture and raise children, a sort of "preparation of the soul by habit" for young people, so that they are conditioned to the right type of likes and dislikes. It is obvious that in the first part of this syllogism, the philosopher accepts the existence of a predisposition by Nature, and in the second, the behavioural rules of learning are followed. Indeed, at another relevant point he specifically mentions the law of reward-or-punishment, when he declares that following an action of ours we will either be praised or blamed.

Hexis can be virtuous; in a laconic definition of virtues Aristotle calls them "among the *hexis* those praiseworthy" (1103a). Habits to be virtuous must fulfil three conditions of conscious effort by the Self: They should not be applied haphazardly, but the person who performs an action must himself choose what he is going to do, should know well his object, and also do that firmly and without hesitation.

CHAPTER TWELVE

Special characteristics according to age and gender

Aristotle divides personality characteristics into two main categories: virtues and vices. His concern is, of course, philosophical; in the *Nicomachean* and *Eudemian Ethics*, moral, to teach men how to become good and virtuous (*agathos*); and social in *Politics*, in order to advise how one can be a good citizen (*polites*). Yet in one of his more analytic descriptions of virtue, there are parameters of psychological interest: Virtue is a characteristic that has been reached after deliberation and choice, which always tends towards the mean—to a middle road relative to us, and which is determined by rational thoughts such as those of a prudent man. The elements in this passage refer at the same time to some psychic potentialities that a virtuous person should possess: freedom of thought, good judgement, self-knowledge, logic, and moral strength.

A fundamental theory in the Aristotelian philosophy is "the rule of the mean", according to which in all phenomena, natural or human, the middle way for actions—rather than the extremes—always brings the best results. Aristotle considers that a personality trait belonging to the categories of virtues is the mean between two vices, the one characterized by excess and the other by deficiency.

A classical example is bravery, its excess being audacity and its deficiency cowardice. In *Eudemian Ethics*, the philosopher presents a table of 14 virtues and their corresponding vices—a total of 42 specific characteristics (1221a). It is psychologically significant that his approach is not impersonal, but on the contrary very human. He himself stresses that the mean in interpersonal relations is not like in mathematics, "where 6 is at an equal distance from 2, as well as 10" (1106b).

The Stagirite advises that when examining personality profiles and generally human affairs there is a need for flexibility. He points out the factor of subjectivity by saying that in such matters the mean does not consist of the parameters of the object per se, but how they relate to us. In psychological characterizations, there is the factor of relativity; for example, a coward considers a brave man as audacious and reckless, while an audacious person calls the same man a coward. The individual differences of how people judge the right mean is correlated by the philosopher with constitution; we were told in a previous chapter (Chapter Nine "The gifts of Nature") that there are constitutional inclinations which differ from person to person, "since each one of us has by Nature tendencies towards other targets" (1109b).

Furthermore, he accepts that maintaining the proper measure in our behaviour is difficult for everybody, and it depends to a large extent on the circumstances—with whom we are dealing, on what subject, for how long, and so forth. There is an excellent paradigm from medicine in the text: Generally, for somebody in fever rest and diet are helpful, but in a particular case, they may not. In addition to the above factors, age and gender determine to a certain degree several special characteristics, which are added to the profile and behaviour of a person (as we will discuss immediately below).

Aristotle's general admonition regarding the virtues, as personality characteristics worthwhile pursuing, is a down-to-earth, practical viewpoint. Virtues, he declares, are not a self-seeking aim, but the tools that we can use and apply in everyday life for our own benefit.

Personality characteristics of young people

Young people are rightly considered by Aristotle as full of desires. We have been previously told, when discussing children's qualities (in Chapter Ten "The effects of the environment"), that appetites and desires are flooding Man's existence during his first years and that reasoning develops later. Young people are still carried away by intense desires, which nevertheless change direction easily and in an unrestrained way. Especially this happens for sexual relations, in which satiation comes quickly, the philosopher remarks.

In *Nicomachean Ethics* the erotic relations of youngsters are described in detail (see also Chapter Fifteen "Erotic love"), and as based on passion and pleasure. There importance is given to sight, as the main sensual function through which lovers are attracted to each other, although the significance of a good character in both is underlined in order for a steady bond to last.

The usually vehement way of reacting leads young persons to an extreme behaviour and, if they feel they have been treated unjustly, they become hot-tempered and full of anger. In fact, the Stagirite uses in *Rhetoric* the adjective "hot-blooded" (*diathermoi*) for youth, explaining that "Nature has made them as if having drunk a lot of wine" (1389a).

The philosopher praises young men for several of their characteristics: for instance, for their love for honour and their efforts to win. They want to be superior without pursuing money—"because they have not experienced poverty" (1389a), is his psychological interpretation. He also says that in general they are of good will and magnanimous, because they have not yet met with cunning people and they have not lived humiliations.

Aristotle considers optimism a main element of youth. He describes young people as hopeful, living everything with fruitful expectations, since the future belongs to them, and because they have not known failures and they have not been deceived by others. That is why he calls them "credulous". In addition, he explains how optimism pushes young men to act with bravery, "since having hopes always gives you courage" (1389a).

For the emotional sphere of young people's life, the Stagirite makes a comprehensive description showing the extreme ways of their age. He aptly remarks that everything is done by them to an excessive degree—they love very much something or somebody, and they hate too much. They love their friends and companions more than the persons of other ages do, and they like to live all day with them. They do not usually criticize their friends, even when their interest is at stake. In a similar excessive and careless way, they make mistakes.

The emotional behaviour of youngsters is full of laughing and joking, since they feel sure of everything. They believe that they are experts on all subjects and so they insist with obstinacy on their views. This sometimes drives them to commit unjust actions, "without any wickedness" (1389b), the philosopher adds.

Personality characteristics of old people

In *Rhetoric*, Aristotle considers that the body of a person is in its prime around the 35th year of age, while the soul until around the 49th. So when he speaks of old people, he most probably means those above the 50th year.

The main axis, which the philosopher follows in his investigation of the personality in old age, is the insecurity gathered with the passing of years. "These people have lived for many years and they have repeatedly been deceived" (1389b) is his psychological explanation; so old age, as he aptly puts it elsewhere, has paved the way for fear and hesitation. He describes old people as being reserved and doubtful in front of everything, so that they frequently express themselves using words like "perhaps" and "maybe".

The emotional condition of old persons being fearful, according to Aristotle, does not allow them to manifest their feelings and they behave in a cold, almost frozen, way. Contrary to younger persons, they do not love or hate intensely and they do not reveal their emotions, especially if they had previously been humiliated. The only thing they want is to survive, the philosopher adds, since "they are conscious of the fact that they are living their last days—and Man craves more for what he is going to lose" (1389b).

Aristotle considers that in view of the above, old persons become suspicious and stingy (in contrast again to younger people), since they have a personal experience of how easily money may be lost and of how difficult it is to earn it back.

Another factor accounting for the insecurity of old age is in some cases a disturbance of memory. In *On Memory*, Aristotle refers to that and the reasons he gives are psychopathologically very correct: The very young and the elderly do not present good memory because they are in a continuous change, the former since they are still in a developing stage, doing everything quickly and so not retaining mnemonic images, and the latter because they are too slow and they cannot imprint new stimuli. Thus, the philosopher has registered what today we call "senile amnesia" of recent events.

Aristotle in *Rhetoric* describes old people as being usually pessimistic, almost depressive, since, as he explains, they have learnt to expect the worse. So they like to live with past memories (and not with any hopes) and they often become very talkative. They also grumble and complain about the present, so that they are not pleasant company and cannot easily make new friends.

Another personality characteristic which changes with age is the expression of anger. According to the philosopher, old persons, although having from time to time outbursts of disagreement, do not keep any available strength in order to act accordingly. In a similar way, their desires and instinctual drives are very weak, in spite of their wishes.

One may gather from most of the above characteristics of senility that Aristotle concentrates on the "negative" elements of that period in human life. Most probably when writing the text he had in mind cases of early senile dementia, which (as we accept today) manifests itself with memory disturbances, depression, paranoid ideas, and behaviour changes of the type described in *Rhetoric*. Nevertheless, in other books, like in *Nicomachean Ethics* and *Politics*, there are references of many "positive" and "good" qualities.

A main asset of old age is the wisdom gained with the years. Nature has bestowed Man with potentialities that are improved in later years—intellectual capacities, correct judgement, better opinions, realistic concepts, and so on. That is why the philosopher advises that "everyone should pay attention to what the elderly say, because even without bringing evidence, they have by experience an eye that sees the right things" (1143b). Elsewhere it is written that Nature has arranged it so that in youth there is physical strength, while in senility prudence and consideration. Weak as they are, old people usually behave in a moderate and self-controlled way. They are also compassionate and pitiful towards other old persons in distress—"since they are afraid they may suffer the same themselves" (1390a) is the philosopher's interpretation.

The above virtuous qualities make old men eligible, Aristotle comments, not only for being the head of their household, but also for having a seat in the senate and other government offices. Old fathers can teach younger members of the family various professions, as well as military tactics. Those of them with musical knowledge can even educate their children on how to play an instrument and thus advance their aesthetic criterion for good melodies!

* * *

Persons in their prime

Persons in their prime are described only shortly by the Stagirite. He believes that a mature person of middle age as a rule chooses the mean between the two extremes that youth and senility may show. For instance, such an individual will behave with courage, but not with audacity or cowardice. And in a rhetoric schema the philosopher closes the description of a mature personality profile: "He is prudent with bravery and brave with prudence" (1390b).

Special characteristics of women

In the discussion of Aristotle's "comparative psychology" (see Chapter Nine "The gifts of Nature"), we have seen that in his book *History of Animals*, among other parameters, he investigated the different behaviour of male and female animals in various species. In the same text and as a continuation of the above he proceeds to an analogous comparison between the personality traits of men and women attributing the differences to innate (biological) dispositions programmed by Nature. He describes women as being more compassionate than men, and as crying more easily. They are more alert to situations and have fewer needs. The philosopher calls women dysthymic and pessimistic, as well as envious, gossiping, and grumbling. He even states that they are more impertinent and lie more frequently than men. Several of the last characterizations were considered by some circles as a diminution of the woman's profile. Nevertheless, that passage does not represent the opinion of Aristotle on the whole. In *Nicomachean Ethics* and *Eudemian Ethics*, he praises on various occasions the character of the woman, especially her role as a wife and as a mother.

In his description of marital relations, the Stagirite clearly indicates the values and contributions of the wife, when he says that from the very beginning the spouses divide their activities, so that they help each other and have satisfactory and sufficient results. This complementary way of acting he regards as being beneficial for both, and above all as a possibility for communication on a mutual basis. Indeed, he believes that the first source of companionship and love is to be found in the household. Furthermore, the fact that he distinguishes Man from animals, stating that mating happens after choosing one's partner, shows that the philosopher considers wives as possessing their own values.

The properties constituting the value of each person may be different, but regarding the woman in her duties as a wife and a mother Aristotle advises that she should get the respect appropriate for her by the husband and the children. Although the philosopher does not make a direct reference to the sexual relations of a married couple, the role of the woman as a lovable and "sweet" person is distinct in the line: "If both partners are good each will delight and find joy in the virtues of the other" (1162a) (see also Chapter Thirteen "Family relations").

Another proof of Aristotle's appreciation for women is his praising words regarding motherhood. He calls mothers "more-loving-the-children" (*philo-teknoterai*) (1168a) than the fathers, ready to sacrifice themselves for the children's sake, feeling as if they are the sole creators of offspring. We have also seen when discussing parental care (Chapter Ten "The effects of the environment") how a mother, irrespective of circumstances, participates in her children's joys and sorrows.

PART IV

INTERPERSONAL RELATIONS

From the adjectives Aristotle used in order to define Man's roles in various situations, it becomes evident that he always had in mind Man's interpersonal relations. He calls Man "*zoon oikonomikon*", in other passages "*zoon politicon*", and elsewhere "*zoon koinonikon*", which means "animal" concerned with household problems, involved in political affairs, and being generally social (and sociable).

We have seen in previous chapters many types of interpersonal relations being discussed by the philosopher from various angles—for example, the way that parents care for their children (Chapter Ten "The effects of the environment"), the behaviour of youngsters towards others (Chapter Twelve "Special characteristics according to age and gender"), and the difficulties of old people to relate to others because of hardships gathered through the years (Chapter Twelve). The emotional interactions between two or more persons are traced and investigated by the Stagirite very efficiently, and with many details regarding their intensity, stability, and so on.

When one reads the books of *Nicomachean* and *Eudemian Ethics* which deal with family relations, friendship, and eros, one gets the feeling that what is being described are scenes of today's everyday life, with people having the same joys, problems, love affairs, and interpersonal difficulties then and nowadays. So Aristotle proves to be a realist studying things the way they are. At the same time, he is an objective observer, with a penetrating eye into the dynamics of human relations.

CHAPTER THIRTEEN

Family relations

Family relations are described in quite some extent in three chapters (Book VIII) of the *Nicomachean Ethics*. Aristotle gives particular importance to the structure and function of the household (*oikos*), as shown in his epigrammatic phrase "the household comes first and is more indispensable than the state (*polis* = city-state)" (1162a). This statement, combined with another in the same text—"Man is by Nature inclined to live in couples rather than as a political being" (1162a)—makes clear the position of the philosopher, who gives more weight to the psychological needs of an individual through intrafamilial relations than his role in the state as a citizen. Such a view is not frequently found in ancient Greek literature, since in those times the duty of a free citizen (*polites*) and generally his life were inseparable from that of the city. Even when Aristotle formulates his classical phrase in the *Eudemian Ethics*—"Man is a sociable (*koinonikon*) animal" (1242a)—a few lines further he completes: "It is in the household that one can find the beginning and the sources of love, of community life and of justice" (1242b).

The above shows the emphasis the philosopher puts on the psychological necessity of people communicating with each other, and how that starts in the family. It also shows how sensitive and receptive he was for human needs.

Fatherly and motherly love

A father's love is much greater than the love of his children for him, according to Aristotle; and, he adds, in the same way the children when grown up will love more their own offspring. He also offers an explanation for this type of relationship: "Because in life to act (*energein*) and produce is always more satisfactory than to remain inactive" (1241b). The philosopher compares fatherly love with that of a good shepherd or a just king. In a similar way, they all take care, provide good things, and confer benefits upon those for whom they are responsible. We have seen when discussing the effect of parental care on the formation of personality (Chapter Ten "The effects of the environment") that the love of the father originates from a biological and psychological feeling of the father that the child is "like a part of himself" and so he is trying to make it prosper, to maintain and educate it.

In spite of the relatively superior position of the father, justice is what governs his relationship with his children, and furthermore what is right is not an absolute value and so it is not in every case the same. With such non-dogmatic views the philosopher stresses the fact that in loving situations what is just must depend on the worth and merit of each person.

A mother's relationship with her children is considered by Aristotle the ideal love, the one that offers everything "in joys and in sorrows" (1166a). The magnitude of love which Aristotle attributes to mothers is shown in the *Nicomachean Ethics* when he compares it as a model for the love between friends. In trying to describe the characteristics of a real and true friend who gives what his partner wishes and does so for the partner's sake, the philosopher says: "in the way it is met to the utmost degree in the case of mothers" (1166a).

In the *Eudemian Ethics*, he underlines maternal devotion and sacrifice, referring to some female animals that prefer to stand in front of the enemy and die in order to save their offspring. In the same text, he repeats what we have discussed in the chapter on parental care; that a mother's love is greater than that of a father's (*philo-teknoterai*) (1168a). He explains that as being a result of the mother's belief that a child is more her own creation, since she actually put greater efforts to feed and raise it. And he concludes that whatever one creates is measured according to how difficult it has been.

Relationships of children

Children's love for their parents is considered by Aristotle a duty they owe to them, "like the one that men owe to Gods" (1162a). Yet he elucidates that children are not obliged to give everything to the parents, "as to Jupiter are not given all kinds of honours and sacrifices" (1244a). He also makes a distinction that other good gestures should be made for a mother and different are those appropriate for a father. The gratitude of the children is because the parents have offered a great lot by rearing and educating them.

The love between children and parents is by far more pleasant than the friendship or love for a stranger outside the family. Parents, Aristotle remarks, love their children since the first day they are born, while the children do so only with the passing of time, when they acquire comprehension and they can value things and situations. In a book like the *Nicomachean Ethics* dealing with moral values, interpersonal relations are examined also from the viewpoint of justice: It is not allowed for a son to disown his father, because he will always be in debt to the latter; nothing a son may do will ever be a worthy return for all his father has provided. Aristotle, nevertheless, recognizes in addition the psychological side of the relation: No father will ever reject or keep away from his son, unless the son is exceedingly wicked; it is natural for a father to be emotionally close to his children.

Love between siblings is, according to the philosopher, primarily related to a biological factor, their common origin, which, however, leads to a psychological identification in many respects. They come from the same "blood and root" (1161b) and the similarity with the parents ends up in a similarity between themselves. "It is as if they are one divided in many (persons)" (1161b). The closer they are in age and the longer they have lived together, the more they love each other.

The influence of the family atmosphere on fraternal interpersonal relations is even more stressed in another passage of the *Nicomachean Ethics*: The fact that the children were raised since their birth and for a long time in the same surroundings with loving parents makes them have an affectionate behaviour to each other. The similar personality characteristics developed in the family environment (*homoetheis*) contribute to a loving relation; that is demonstrated, Aristotle contends, by the fact that between brothers who have a great difference in age a friendly, affectionate relation cannot be expected.

The Stagirite compares brotherly love with a type of friendship of excessive closeness (*hetairiki*). If a young member of a family has an outside friend of around the same age, with similar emotional reactions and identical everyday activities, then they both delight in their company—they become bosom companions. When they are virtuous in character and are more alike generally, they become closely linked and their friendship reaches the level of brotherly love. Real and true friendships of this kind, the philosopher underlines, are very rare and can happen only between two persons and not among many; "it is the type celebrated in hymns" (1171a).

The relation of family members to their cousins is also dealt with by Aristotle. He says that the bond between relatives exists always, especially for those nearer the leader of the family. They all have a common descent and they are all interested in family affairs, so they should be invited and should meet on various occasions such as marriages and funerals.

Husband–wife relations

The husband rules in a family according to his worth and what befits a man who is capable of many things. Yet Aristotle recognizes that the husband must allow for the woman in the family to handle any matters that are appropriate for her. But, he adds, if the husband wants to control everything, then he slips into the mentality of oligarchy because he no more rules by virtue. Very interesting is the immediately next observation of the philosopher, which is very realistic from a psychosocial point of view: When a woman inherits a great fortune, she is the one that rules, based no more on her merit but on power.

In a comprehensive passage of the *Nicomachean Ethics*, the Stagirite presents three aspects of the husband–wife association: the biological, the sociological, and the emotional. He states that it is programmed by Nature for man and woman to be attracted and to live as a couple. Nevertheless, contrary to what happens in animals in which procreation for conservation of the species is the ultimate and only biological goal, humans live under the same roof planning their lives, sharing their duties for a common cause, and contributing to each other's needs so that they can all have a better life in the society (*koinonia*). The structure of the family, therefore, and the relationship between husband and wife are not only useful, but also produce the prerequisites for intrafamilial communication (*koinonia*—a word with a double meaning).

The psychological side of the husband–wife bond is stressed in the *Eudemian Ethics*, where Aristotle discriminates two types of friendship or love, the one coming from common blood and the other because of knowing one another in life. "In contrast to the animals which mate with anyone of the opposite gender by chance" (1242a), humans have the ability of choice. So the emotional attachment of the couple becomes pleasant—"sweet" (1162a) is the word the philosopher uses in the *Nicomachean Ethics*, where he adds a very eloquent phrase: "If both partners are good, each will delight and find joy in the virtues of the other" (1162a). Interestingly, there is no reference in the Aristotelian vocabulary to any word denoting sexual or other somatic relation concerning husband and wife; *erotic*, or the verb *eran* are used in other parts of the book in the case of different types of lovers (see Chapter Fifteen "Erotic love").

* * *

The reader will have noticed that Aristotle in his investigation of the intrafamilial relations—those of the father, the mother, the siblings, the cousins, the husband, or the wife—covers all subjects by approaching them from various angles. His keen observation, irrespective of the main scope of the book he is writing, registers many aspects of interpersonal associations which are of interest to psychology and which can be categorized into three types: biological, sociopolitical, and psychological.

The biological element is evident in all cases. The philosopher mentions it as the original source on which the family bonds are based. "By Nature" (*physei*) (1161a), by a natural drive, the father loves his children, the mother feels her children are part of herself, the siblings have a common origin, husband and wife are destined to live as a couple, and so on.

The sociopolitical aspect results from the Stagirite's concern for a well-governed state. Since in many of his books (and as a principal subject in *Politics*) the philosopher examines in detail the pros and cons of the political systems in many Greek cities–states, and since he believes that the household comes before the state, his comparisons of some intrafamilial relations with political conditions are to be expected: A father's love is the same as that of a good king; a parent should not become a tyrant; a wife must not act like politicians in oligarchies, and so on. Justice should rule in a house, like in society, and each should get what they are worthy of. The solidarity of relatives is important, so that the structure of the family is strong and its function in the society secures the everyday needs of life. Frequent meetings of family members on various social occasions contribute to the above.

The psychological characteristics of family relations in the Aristotelian texts have already been presented in this chapter: the continuous love and care of the father; the devotion of the mother; the "sweet" emotional bonds existing in couples; and so on. Interesting psychodynamically is the note about identification of the parents with the children and similarity of personality with consequent affection between siblings when brought up together. An analogous view is expressed by Aristotle in his discussion about the determining factors for friendship (see Chapter Fourteen "Friendship"): *isotes—homeotes—philotes* (equality—similarity—friendship), which means that under the same conditions and similar personality traits a better friendship will be established. Other noticeable references of emotional manifestations are made for all family members, underlining the joy they get when they share together various good things.

CHAPTER FOURTEEN

Friendship

Friendship is a fundamental interpersonal relation for all ages in every society.

The Aristotelian key words characterizing friendship are contained in a laconic sentence: "All kinds of friendship exist by interrelating/intercommunicating" (1161b). *En koinonia* is the ancient Greek expression having, as one can gather from the detailed descriptions later, a double meaning: psychological—to participate, to communicate feelings, ideas, and so on with others; and sociological—to have things in common, to act in common. (*Koinonia* in modern Greek means "society", and in the Greek Orthodox Church "Holy Communion".)

The psychosocial necessity for friendship

An important view of Aristotle at the beginning of Book VIII of the *Nicomachean Ethics* is that friendship is most indispensable in life, since nobody would prefer to live without friends, even if he had all the goods at his disposal. The philosopher enumerates many categories of people needing friends, explaining also the reasons for that. The rich and those in power require friendship in order to keep their prosperity, while people in poverty or suffering misfortune can find refuge only in friends. In addition, the young need friends in order to avoid mistakes and sins, as well as persons in their prime to be reminded of and proceed to noble actions, and old people to be helped in whatever they cannot anymore achieve. The Stagirite extends his view even further—friendship is necessary for fellow-citizens in order for their state to be held together safe; in this way the wise lawgivers take care more of the concord between fellow-men than they do for justice.

In the text, there are some interesting comments of the ancient philosopher, which show how interpersonal relations are the same throughout the ages: "Even when one travels abroad, one understands how dear and friendly every man is to some others" and "Having many friends is one of the best things in life" (1155a).

There has always been a question whether in friendship one seeks for somebody like him (in age, character, etc.), or on the contrary if people who are alike are jealous and antagonize each other. Previous philosophers and theatrical writers tried to give theoretical answers or answers based on physical phenomena, while Aristotle, following his usual realistic and down-to-earth approach, based on objective observations, places the problem on a more human level, taking into consideration the variety of emotions and personalities (*pathe* and *ethe*). So he asks himself whether all people, good and bad, can be friendly, if there is one kind of friendship or more, and so on.

Types of friendship and their aims

Aristotle begins to investigate the parameters of friendship based on psychological motives and final aims. He considers that a lovable object or person worthy of our friendship is only that which is good (*agathon*), pleasant (*hedy*), or useful (*chresimon*)—thus defining three types of friendship. He furthermore adds that we regard something as useful if it helps us to obtain something else good or pleasant—something lovable—as such constituting our final aim. The philosopher proceeds to analyse what is meant by *agathon*, approaching the subject on a psychological level without any idealistic or theocratic theories. To the question of whether men love the generally good or what is good for themselves—underlining the fact that the two do not always agree—he concludes that everyone at the end prefers and loves what is good for himself. Yet the Stagirite does not remain content with this point of analysis and goes even further to a deeper psychological statement: "Everyone loves not what is in reality good for him, but what appears to him to be good" (1155b). So without making any moral comments (as other philosophers might do) on such aspects of human behaviour, Aristotle accepts the individuality and subjectivity of feelings in human interpersonal relations, conditions which affect the development of friendships.

Aristotle is interested in the ways that a stable friendship can be achieved. Without hiding his preference for the friendship with good as its objective, he does not reject as absolutely unacceptable the other two types of friendship—with pleasure or usefulness as their aim—but regards these two as having disadvantages. He explains this last view of his, making at the same time very apt psychological comments. He remarks, for instance, that those who become friends because of usefulness do not actually feel affection for each other, but are befriending each other to gain something; the same is true for those whose motive is pleasure. So in both of these types of friendship one does not love the other for being *the kind of person he really is,* but for something useful or pleasant. Such types of friendship the philosopher rightly calls "incidental" and easily dissolved: he notes that people with such personalities are changeable; their needs in life become in the course of time different; and since there are no more lovable motives for them, the friendship ceases to exist.

Aristotle, stressing the importance of subjectivity in the feelings during a friendship, underlines the necessity for a fundamental attitude of each partner in order for the stability and lengthy duration of the bond: One should wish and act for the good of one's friend *for the friend's sake.* And in order to succeed in that, the philosopher advises that one should have good will and should be aware of the feelings, disposition, and needs of the other.

In other passages of the *Nicomachean Ethics* Aristotle returns again to his opinion that friendships with the ultimate purpose of profit cannot last long. The main reason is that such friendships are not based on the recognition of each partner's personality as good, and so there is no trust between the two parts. The philosopher, nevertheless, accepting the realities of human psychology does not exclude good men from seeking friendships for pleasure, and not only that, he remarks that in such cases friendships can be more stable if they are based on good personalities ready to offer. Another disadvantage of a friendship for profit is mentioned in the text: quarrels and complaints arise, as it would be expected, since each friend demands more and more from the other claiming that he does not get what he deserves.

Determining conditions for friendship

Aristotle's diligent study of interpersonal relations led him to formulate some determining conditions under which a real and stable friendship can develop. Of course, as we have already seen, he believes that a fundamental basis is a good and virtuous personality, but he is not dealing with the subject only from a moral aspect, nor is he ending in praises or criticism for anyone. Indeed, he succeeds in giving evidence for his views with examples from everyday life—one more proof of the philosopher's ability to approach human behaviour from a psychological viewpoint.

One of the foremost prerequisites for a sound and stable friendship according to Aristotle is reciprocity. A mutual give-and-take strengthens the bonds between friends. The philosopher's opinion, on which he insists, is that as there are three types of friendship, each with its different lovable aim, the friends should be aware of that and willing to help one another toward a relevant kind of aim. So reciprocity should be directed according to the motives and objectives of the partner. In the text there is a phrase that can be considered a definition of friendship: "Friendship exists when good will and favour are mutual" (1155b). This condition can be secured, according to the philosopher, only by mature and good (*agathoi*) persons, since they act like that for their own sake too, because it is part of their beliefs. On the contrary, foolish and frivolous persons can make only incidental and transient friendships.

Another condition that Aristotle considers essential for the establishment of the right kind of friendship is trust between friends. Then the friendship will be unbreakable, since neither of the people involved will believe any slander from a third person. Also they will not be unjust to each other. For this condition to be achieved, the philosopher remarks that time is needed, so that friends will live common experiences and get accustomed to each other's habits—something extremely difficult. Continuing to elaborate on human relations from a psychodynamic angle, Aristotle notes that distances do not dissolve friendships, they only suspend common activities for a period—unless the separation becomes permanent and then the friendship is forgotten.

At the same time, Aristotle underlines the need for common interests and common objects of joy in order for a friendship to last. For that reason, in another passage of the *Nicomachean Ethics*, where he enumerates the determining conditions for friendship, he includes similarity (*home-otes*), at least to a certain extent, regarding habits and trends of personality. Probable disagreements are surpassed with time—and the philosopher for this occasion cites a proverb: "... after the friends have consumed salt" (1156b) (in modern Greek we say "bread and salt"). In *Eudemian Ethics* he repeats the same views, yet he accepts that dissimilar characters may also be attracted to each other. He says: "People do not amuse themselves only by seeking nice food, but because they are looking for pleasant company" (1244b) and "It is a need for some to find a person like them, but others are searching for the opposite—like the dry earth that loves rain" (1235a).

The psychological individuality of each person is respectable in the Aristotelian philosophy without any pompous statements. So the Stagirite simply advises that since a friendship is established for both friends' sake, each partner should consider the individual choices of the other and, wherever possible, follow the latter's wishes. There is a whimsical note in the *Eudemian Ethics*: "A person loves his friend for the latter's friendship and for the pleasure the friend chooses to give, that is, loves him as a friend and ... not as if the friend were a musician or a physician" (1237b).

As a consequence of the aspects of friendship just mentioned, and chiefly of the fact that each friend should make an equal return for the good he enjoyed from his partner, the philosopher in *Nicomachean Ethics* speaks of equality among friends. Since, due to various conditions, equality with equal give-and-take is not easily achieved, Aristotle in *Eudemian Ethics* proceeds to elaborate on the subject and gives realistic and down-to-earth solutions. For instance, instead of *equal return* he proposes *an equivalent return*, analogous to what one has been given. His examples from parallel fields are convincing: A farmer cannot give to a shoemaker exactly the things he takes from him, so in exchange he will give products of his own in analogy. The same holds true for somebody who teaches wisdom and in return takes money (although, the philosopher adds, science and money can never be equalized by the same measure).

Following the above observations and syllogisms, Aristotle phrases a triad containing his views about the determining factors: *philo-tes, iso-tes,* and *homeo-tes,* which mean "friendship", "equality", and "similarity".

Apart from the two kinds of friendship in interpersonal relations—equality and by analogy—the Stagirite describes a third one, in which one of the partners is superior to the other. As such, he mentions the good relations between a ruler and his subjects, or a benefactor and the beneficiary. Nevertheless, he does not consider this kind of relation to be true friendship, because a main determining condition is lacking—that of equal or equivalent return. He also adds a psychological observation—that as a rule persons choosing to make friendships in order to feel superior are the ambitious who want to be admired. Such are persons with a noble descent, or with a difference in age that gives them an advantage over the partner.

In spite of the complexity of the subject, Aristotle does not leave his realistic approach and in *Eudemian Ethics* registers also cases of dissimilar friendships, at the same time criticizing them as being easily dissolved. For instance, he characterizes a friendship based on usefulness as one which many a time is for the self-interest of one partner only and can be saved solely by legal actions. For those who start a friendship only to get pleasure and nothing else, each with his own aims, the philosopher says "they quickly get rid of each other" (1245a). Yet he does not condemn pleasure as such and in its general sense. He elucidates his view by stating that in friendships of virtuous people there is a mutual choice of good things, which can at the same time be pleasant. He even connects in these cases the good and pleasant by saying that in the first and foremost type of friendship one feels pleasure as a result of the virtuous atmosphere of the relation.

The adjectives used in the Aristotelian texts for the "good and virtuous" (*agathe kat' areten*) friendship, which the philosopher evidently prefers and indirectly proposes, are numerous: "perfect", "highest", "best", "permanent", "reasonable", "assured". There is an epigrammatic phrase in *Eudemian Ethics*: "Real friends are one soul" (1240b); and in *Nicomachean Ethics*: "To be loved in a friendship seems to be preferable than receiving honours" (1159a). Of course, admitting that such a friendship is only very rarely acquired, Aristotle accepts the realities in human psychology and notes how some people enjoy for a while a good time with another person by a somatic, hedonistic relation, or somebody else by participating in music teaching, or still others by … philosophizing.

The importance of character

From what has been discussed up to now it is obvious that Aristotle gives great importance not only to the motives and objectives of a friendship, but also to the personality and its ability (or not) to offer in an interpersonal relation. He differentiates emotions from characteristics of the personality necessary for the establishment of a real friendship. Affections or sympathy are emotions that can be felt also for inanimate objects, while mutual friendship requires the ability to choose, which depends on the characteristics of personality; we have already seen that friends should wish the best for their partner's sake, something determined not by emotions but by a good character. At the beginning of Book IX of *Nicomachean Ethics* the importance of character is strongly emphasized (in an almost poetic way): "Friendship based on the personality is lasting, since it exists for the sake of love itself" (1164a).

On the contrary, when a friendship is not based on good personalities, but one partner looks how to get the other's belongings (which, the philosopher underlines, can change any minute to the worse), then there is no more partnership. In the Aristotelian texts, there are descriptions of many types of personality that lead a friendship to dissolution. Here only a few will be cited.

In *Nicomachean Ethics*, Aristotle draws the characteristics of hypocrites pretending to love their friend for his good behaviour and manners, while they want to exploit him or are only after pleasure; in such cases, the philosopher advises that the good friend can complain and denounce the relationship.

In the case of persons who turn out to be evil, the Stagirite puts the question of whether one should immediately break off the friendship. His answer is very interesting since it shows a psychotherapeutic, I would say, intention: If there is a possibility to correct the wickedness of such persons, one should help them so that they improve their personality—unless they are incurable. He concludes that it is better to reform them than, say, help them increase their property, since personality is an integral part of friendship.

Another example of interpersonal relation destined to be dissolved is that in which with the passing of years one of the friends has changed in character, and so the other keeps away. This may happen in childhood friendships, when one remains childish in the way he thinks, while the other becomes a mature personality. It is natural, Aristotle remarks, that the two no more like or enjoy the same things. Yet the philosopher makes a human comment: The former friend should not be treated as if he had never been a friend, but one should show some affection for him for the sake of old friendship.

In *Eudemian Ethics* Aristotle extends his investigation to possible friendships between villain persons. Each one of them is after his own interest and pleasure and may be patient for a period of time, but when they both start being unjust and hurting each other, they cannot any longer be called friends. The philosopher then proceeds to a psychological interpretation: a villain man is distrustful and malignant because as a measure for the rest he uses what he himself is.

Aristotle, in spite of his preference for virtuous friendships (one must not forget that *Nicomachean Ethics* and *Eudemian Ethics* are, first of all—as the titles denote—books about morality), does not hesitate to study without any prejudice the interpersonal relations between opposing characters. He brings the example of a good man who from time to time may be on friendly terms with a villain, if the latter serves a particular aim, away from wicked actions. For instance, the other may be a good musician and they may both enjoy his kind of music. People, the philosopher concludes, can adapt to each other's needs because there is in all men a part that is good—some kind of virtue in everybody. This last opinion shows how objectively and without prejudice Aristotle examined interpersonal relations, as well as his psychological ability to penetrate into the complicated nature of the human personality, accepting the co-existence of both positive and negative traits.

In *Eudemian Ethics*, there is a very interesting proposal for discussion of a rather philosophical and ethical subject, but one at the same time psychological. The Stagirite asks whether one should demand from his friend to suffer with him when he is suffering a misfortune. His answers are the two extremities of the subject, although they come from actual happenings in life: Somebody who really loves his friend would not want to involve him in miseries, even if the friend is ready and willing to participate; a good man does not choose to find joy in the compassion of a friend, restraining himself to his own problems—the philosopher says. On the other hand, he describes among other cases the following, quite opposite to the previous, which he himself calls the worst: a person in misery does not tolerate his friend if the latter is joyful and happy (for his own reasons) and kills him, committing shortly afterwards suicide!

Aristotle at some point raises a crucial issue: Is it possible to recognize who is a real and true friend? Instead of giving his personal answer, he prefers to refer to what various groups of people would believe. For instance, some people, presumably the easy-going, think that it is not difficult to find a good friend, while others that you can only rarely do so and only during a period of misfortune in which a friend can be tested. Still others, more suspicious in character, do not trust a new friend even if he is helping in a new problem, because they believe that he may be pretending in order to gain something in later, happier days. One will notice that the attitudes registered by the philosopher are determined by the personality of the individuals in each group.

* * *

Friendship, a fundamental interpersonal relation, is approached by Aristotle from many angles. As we have seen, he distinguishes various types of friendship, as well as a great number of personalities—virtuous (good, decent, tolerant, grateful, with good will) and non-virtuous (evil, wicked, villain, distrustful, suspicious, incontinent), each entering into a different kind of friendly relation and bond. The importance of personality is comprehensively expressed in *Eudemian Ethics*: The ability for friendship originates from a trait of the personality. The philosopher elaborates on that a little later distinguishing two groups of people: Those who are predisposed to love and be affectionate, and those who are selfish and only want to be loved. The latter seek admiration by their environment and become "friends by superiority", while the former are glad when there is a chance for them to offer love—it is as if "there is an inner need to act so" (1239a).

CHAPTER FIFTEEN

Erotic love

Aristotle describes erotic love in the chapters of *Nicomachean Ethics* in which he examines the subject of friendship. Indeed the definition he gives to this type of love is made in comparison to friendship; a laconic definition: "Being in love (*eros*) is a kind of excessive friendship" (1171a). He explains this similarity by adding that in both friendship and love a person cannot have a close bond with more than one. It is a fact of life, he says, that an erotic love should be unique, like it happens in bosom companions.

Youth and erotic drives

The Stagirite connects erotic love with youth. His arguments are based on the similar behaviour of young people with that of those in love. In doing so, he proves himself remarkably observant regarding age changes and emotional conditions: Young people are inclined to get in love driven mostly by their emotions and passion. Their aim is pleasure, as it happens in friendships of youngsters. In both cases, these bonds are often temporary and feelings may change within one day following what the moment brings. Yet with the passing of years, tastes change and consequently different kinds of associations are sought. Young men become friends or get in love quickly, while old men do not.

Aristotle attributes to Nature the excessive type of feelings between lovers and the fact that in *eros* an individual is guided (again by Nature, *pe-phyken*) to show the greatest affection towards only one person. An individual cannot be emotionally committed to many persons, because it is not easy to find them all the very best and the very pleasing. The role of the erotic drives given by Nature is stressed by the philosopher in a passage in which he considers a sensory function, that of sight, as the one participating energetically for erotic attraction between two persons. For people in love seeing one another is what pleases them the most, and they prefer this sense to any other. Indeed, he concludes, through seeing, *eros* is first generated and later is supported to exist.

The sensual–instinctual dimension of *eros* is evident moreover from the verbs Aristotle uses for the subject in *Eudemian Ethics*. The nouns *orexis* (appetite) and *epithymia* (desire) are used interchangeably in the discussion about erotic love, as well as their corresponding verbs, thus denoting the intense and vehement quality of this type of emotional condition. We have seen in the chapter about volition (Chapter Four "Volition [will] and psychomotor function") that in the Aristotelian texts those nouns correspond greatly to the instinctual drives of today's psychology. *Orexis*-appetite is an innate function with great impetus, expressing internal needs, which ask for immediate satisfaction at any cost, in an impulsive or even irrational way. *Epithymia*-desire, according to Aristotle's definition, is the appetitive seeking of sweet pleasure (*hedone*) and it acts against reason. A characteristic passage demonstrates the antithesis between the instinctual desire-for-pleasure and the conscious wish (*voulesis*) for good (*agathon*) in the case of erotic love. A lover, says the philosopher, is one who is all the time in love, and if he intensely desires then his purpose is to get hedonistic pleasure from the beloved. However, if he has reasonable wishes, then it is for the good of both, because, Aristotle adds, "*hedone* and *agathon* are two different things" (1235b).

A distinction is made by the Stagirite between erotic love and simple friendship based on the existence or not of sensual desire. For instance, he notes that a person in love is driven by appetitive desires to live under the same roof with his beloved, in which case he does not do it in a proper way, but mainly in order "to satisfy his senses" (*kat' aesthesin*) (1245a). We have already been told of the role of sight in giving pleasure; sexual relation is only seldom mentioned.

The subject of hedonistic pleasure in general (*hedone*) is extensively discussed in *Nicomachean Ethics* (Books VII and X), mainly from a philosophical aspect—whether *hedone* is "good (*agathon*) or bad (*kakia*)". Among the arguments, we can find some that have psychological interest: Young people, because of their continuous growing up, are in an excited condition like that of a drunkard, they are all the time in an appetitive desire and consequently they pursue pleasure as a medicine (*iatreia*). So, "youth is by itself full of pleasure" (1156b). The philosopher is of the opinion that not only youngsters, but everybody, to a point, enjoys food, wine, and sexual relations (*aphrodisia*), because he considers them necessary pleasures. (In fact they are necessary as they serve the psychobiological functions of nutrition and reproduction—see Chapter Eight "Nutrition and reproduction".) The conclusion is typical of Aristotelian philosophy avoiding the extremes: Bodily pleasures are not bad by themselves, but only when excessively sought, which happens in the case of wicked people; then they are not only bad, but also harmful and reproachable.

Many people prefer bodily pleasures, among which the erotic, for various reasons. One is, according to Aristotle, the ability of pleasure to expel emotional pain. The more extreme the unhappiness and distress of a man, the more he is after bodily pleasures, which are thus considered remedial. Another reason is that the pleasures of the body, forceful as they are, can satisfy persons who are otherwise unable to pursue other types of pleasures, such as intellectual. The philosopher brings as an example those frivolous and foolish individuals who live as parasites in the courts of tyrants offering amusements and indulging in bodily pleasures.

Emotional issues in love affairs

In addition to the role of Nature through beautiful looks and instinctual drives, for a love affair to begin, other, mainly emotional, elements must be present in order for an erotic bond to develop and become stable. That is why Aristotle declares that for a true *eros*, pleasure derived only from seeing is not sufficient; real love exists if one is full of feelings and desire for the other when the latter is absent, and if he craves for their meeting again. So the philosopher takes it for granted that as communication is basic for any friendship, it is more so for erotic love. The lovers prefer to live together and when they have common interests, the love affair develops more smoothly.

Aristotle proceeds to examine the problems that not infrequently arise between lovers. He points out the temporary nature of beauty in youth, differentiating the opposing roles and purposes that sometimes exist between the lover and the beloved. They do not always take pleasure from the same things, he says. For instance, if the lover is seeking only the pleasure from the beautiful appearance of the other, and if the beloved is asking for continuous care, then with the passing of years interpersonal conditions may change. The face of the beloved may not be attractive anymore, while he also may not be satisfied from the changing behaviour of the lover. Sometimes quarrels start from the moment that lovers become conscious of the fact that their purposes in getting in-love were different from the very beginning.

Like in the dissimilar friendships, in love affairs if the lover is emotionally very expressive and the beloved is only after usefulness, then the former will complain that the latter does not respond to their feelings, while the beloved will start grumbling that what was originally promised is no longer given. Such love affairs, the philosopher remarks, with different motives and only the self-interest (and not for the partner's sake) are destined eventually, sooner or later, to be dissolved. There is a degree of satire in a paragraph of the text where it is written that even ugly (and probably older) lovers demand to be loved the way that they used to be. If they are otherwise lovable, the philosopher comments, they deserve to receive affections, but if not they become socially ridiculous. At another point, he condemns those who are only after profit and calls them hucksters of love.

In order to underline the importance of character in erotic associations, the Stagirite mentions the case of lovers who, although originally dissimilar, then, by living together and becoming more familiar with each other, accept each other's behaviour and traits and come to please the partner the way that he expects. Therefore, in some respects, they become *homoetheis*, and the love affair remains durable.

Emotional relations between lovers at times take a difficult and disagreeable turn and some weak personalities are easily disappointed and attempt suicide. Aristotle is openly against such an action irrespective of the outcome of the relation. In a chapter about courage in *Nicomachean Ethics* (Book III) he states that "for a man to try to die, because he cannot endure poverty, sadness or an unhappy love affair, is not a characteristic of a courageous person but of a coward; it shows softness to run away from difficult and troublesome conditions" (1116a). In *Eudemian Ethics,* Aristotle illustrates the strong and impulsive erotic drives of malicious persons where he describes how such persons, when in misfortune, do not tolerate their lover remaining alive and finding happiness elsewhere, and so they kill him and then commit suicide!

The bio-psycho-social aspects

Aristotle's approach is global in the sense that he examines people's feelings and activities covering most bio-psycho-social aspects.

The philosopher directly expresses the biological dimension of erotic love when he says that Nature pushes Man to get in love, and that specifically Man is driven by a natural urge towards only one person and not many. He also indicates the way of the original attraction as something somatic, the sight, without neglecting to remind us that the beauty of youth is temporary, since Nature leads us eventually to senility. Sexual relations are mentioned as necessary pleasures, which nevertheless are practiced in excess by disturbed personalities.

The psychological part of *eros'* examination by Aristotle includes both the feelings between lovers as well as the examination of various types of personality. Feelings range, as we have seen, from passionate love to lethal disappointment, from care and devotion to grumbling and fighting, from craving for the absent lover to quick changes of intentions in youngsters, and so forth. The philosopher criticizes some types of personality, for example, those he calls wicked, malicious, frivolous, hedonistic, hucksters, and others, as responsible for leading an erotic association to dissolution.

As a main and determining factor for a stable and lasting love affair, the Stagirite considers the sound personality that has certain features—very near those that are also important for a true friendship: good will from both sides; not having opposing motives; fair give-and-take; common tastes not ignoring the partner's side; and belief in the same values. So the behaviour of each lover should follow in fact the same rules as if in friendship: equality (*iso-tes*) and similarity (*homeo-tes*) which support love and companionship (*philo-tes*). The most successful love affair, therefore, would be the one based on personalities that are *homo-etheis*, that is, with similar traits. Indeed Aristotle suggests the "virtuous similarity" (*kat' areten homeotes*) (1159a) as an ideal association. That does not mean that one partner's personality is flattened in order to get more close to the personality of the other, or that he does not keep his more personal qualities, but it indicates that virtuous persons can harmonize their needs and potentialities with those of the loved one. In this way, the philosopher accepts that even dissimilarity in some aspects does not exclude the possibility of a durable erotic bond. In a realistic approach, he contends that familiarity can decrease differences and in living together each lover can make if not an equal return, an equivalent one.

The social aspect is evident in the discussion of other issues of *eros* by Aristotle. For instance, he considers a satisfactory communication (*koinonia*) necessary between lovers as a fundamental part of their relation; that happens only if they have also common viewpoints about everyday life in the society (*koinonia*, again). Their behaviour should not exceed certain limits, and if one of them would like to impress many in order to erotically attract them, that would mean the beginning of the end for the original relationship. The philosopher makes referrals to other cases, like those of persons living as parasites in the society, others who start an affair for profit, and still others who become socially ridiculous. An extreme, antisocial action condemned by everybody in the society is the killing of one lover by the other, mentioned in the *Eudemian Ethics*.

PART V

PSYCHOANALYTIC CONCEPTS AND ARISTOTLE'S PSYCHOLOGY

In many of the chapters up to now, we have seen not only the psychological aspects that Aristotle brings to surface, but also a psychodynamic approach about which it is worthwhile to elaborate further. In so doing, one is astonished when one comes across observations, ideas, and theories of the philosopher that remind us of and are very close to psychoanalytic concepts. When discussing "volition", for instance, we have met the description of desires and appetites in Aristotelian texts to fulfil the properties of instinctual drives of psychoanalysis; in the chapter on consciousness there is a parallel way of thinking on behalf of the Stagirite with what psychoanalysis considers latent and manifest dreams; the struggle between *orexis* and *logos* is very similar to what today we call "intrapsychic conflict"; and so on.

In the following pages I intend to summarize some such concepts that have already been analysed in previous chapters, and then proceed to discuss in more detail some other notions common (although, of course, not identical) to both the Aristotelian philosophy and the psychoanalytic theory (narcissism, pleasure-*hedone*, etc.).

This attempt is made with all due respect to the logical rules and the conclusive ability of the ancient philosopher, while in no way one would contend that Freud's ideas have been foreseen by Aristotle, but in many issues there exists a corresponding way of thinking by both which makes a relevant discussion worthwhile.

CHAPTER SIXTEEN

Some basic psychoanalytic concepts

Instinctual drive is defined in *The Language of Psycho-analysis* by Laplanche and Pontalis (1985; my emphasis) as "a *dynamic process* consisting of a pressure (charge of *energy*) which *directs* the organism towards an *aim*". We have seen when discussing volition (Chapter Four "Volition [will] and psychomotor function") that Aristotle in his work *On the Soul* in a similar way expresses the role of *orexis* (appetite), containing all the above qualities in one passage: "Appetite is an *active process*, with *energy*, giving a *direction* towards what it desires (towards the *orecton*)" (433b; my emphasis). *Orecton* is the desirable object, which gives pleasure and alleviates psychic pain. So the addition existing in the psychoanalytic definition that "through an object the instinct achieves its aim, that is, to eliminate the state of tension" (Laplanche & Pontalis, 1985), and consequent unpleasure, is also fulfilled in the Aristotelian passage.

Furthermore, the fact that in the psychoanalytic theory the instinct is considered to have its source in bodily stimuli is also mentioned by Aristotle about *orexis*, in the lines just following the above passage: "That which is motivated and directed is the animal and the instrument which appetite employs to produce a move is bodily" (433b). Under the instinctual appetites and desires, the Stagirite includes what psychoanalysis calls ego-instincts of self-preservation when he says: "Hunger and thirst are also desires" (414b). It is noteworthy that the philosopher having a psychobiological approach adds: "Hence the examination of all these falls within the province of the functions common to body and soul" (433b).

Pleasure principle, according to Laplanche and Pontalis (1985), is "one of the two principles governing mental functioning and its psychic activity is aimed at avoiding unpleasure and procuring pleasure"—the other being the *reality principle.* Aristotle points to the same (and continuous) tendency of the desires in human beings to seek for something pleasurable and hedonistic, in contrast to the rational thinking by *logos,* which is always correct and takes into consideration the existing reality (see Chapter Three "Thought and judgement"). Indeed the philosopher stresses the fact that "Nature made us more inclined to pleasure (*hedone*), and therefore to self-indulgence" (1109a); "The living organism is naturally endowed with predispositions which treat pleasure as a guiding principle" is the corresponding phrase in *The Language of Psychoanalysis.* In the ancient text there is even a note that there are individual differences from person to person regarding the search for pleasure (see Chapter Nine "The gifts of Nature")—what today we would call constitutional differences.

Aristotle makes some more interesting remarks. The children live according to their *orexis* and the desire for pleasure largely exists in them since their birth, while only much later does logical thinking try to prevail (see Chapter Ten "The effects of the environment"). To the question sometimes put by psychoanalysts of whether pleasurable tensions do exist, there is an indirect answer in *Nicomachean Ethics* that in some people "the desire for pleasure is greedy and insatiable, and even during the active gratification of appetites their innate drive increases" (1119b).

The structural theory (or second topography) of psychoanalysis distinguishes three parts of the psychic apparatus: the Ego, the Id, and the Superego. Aristotle, on the other hand, divides the particles of *psyche* according to whether they follow logic into two, the rational and the irrational part. We have seen in more detail in Chapter Eleven "The responsibility of one's Self" that the irrational contains the vegetative drives (nutrition and reproduction) and the appetites-desires. All these drives (*hormai* = impulsive forces) have properties found correspondingly in *the Id*, the contents of which "are an expression of the instincts, are unconscious and a portion of them is hereditary and innate" (Laplanche & Pontalis, 1985). The fact that *hormai* of the Aristotelian texts are also considered innate is shown in *Nicomachean Ethics* where it is written: "they are found in embryos as well as in fully grown organisms" (1102a). The observation of Aristotle that "these forces seem to be more active during sleep" (1102b), indicates that their energy originates at an unconscious level.

The rational part is divided by the philosopher into two, the first being the "main and strictly logical" (1102b). The principal function of this part is to restrict the irrational desires, so that "they are disciplined in a prudent man by the action of reason" (1102b); this reminds us of the main role of *the Ego*, which is that of "a mediator, responsible for the interests of the person as a whole", according to Laplanche and Pontalis (1985), and which "defends the person from the claims of the Id".

The second part of the rational element does not bear a name in the ancient text, but it is described as "a part which exists as if listening to the father's commands" (1103a) and that "desires and appetites have to obey to reason, as if to a father's logic" (1102b). Since according to Freud *the Superego* is constituted through the internalization of parental prohibitions and demands and since we know that it judges critically, the proximity of the philosopher's way of thinking is obvious.

Intrapsychic conflict according to psychoanalysis occurs between the Id and the Ego and Superego. In the Aristotelian philosophy, the opposing parts leading to conflicts are the rational *logos* and the irrational desires. Aristotle's laconic phrase "Reason and desires run contrary to each other" (433b) is found in many passages. We have dealt with this subject more extensively in a relevant section of Chapter Eleven "The responsibility of one's Self", but it would be of interest to underline some of the philosopher's opinions. It is important, for instance, that he stresses the forceful energy of the appetites that activate the animalistic part of Man. It is difficult to avoid comparing this with the impetus of the instinctual Id. Even more so when he says that the desires ask for an immediate satisfaction, ignoring the future and carrying away many people—unless by deliberation (conscious thinking) one restrains himself.

Mechanisms of defence are implied in many of Aristotle's works, showing his keen observation ability regarding human behaviour. The mechanism of repression, for instance, is evident in the way that the day's mental processes (thoughts, images, etc.) are referred in his treatise *On Dreams* as being "expelled in depth in the mind" (460b) and "retained in a latent condition" (*On Divination of Sleep*, 463a). We have a little before met the identification with the father and the internalization of his commands. Projection is found in the description of evil and suspicious people who judge others according to their own defects.

Free-association is a method discovered by Freud and used during psychoanalytic therapy; it is based on the fact that when one speaks freely and without consciously selecting his thoughts and words, concealed unconscious ideas, associated to each other, come to the surface in their own order. Aristotle speaks about something very similar when he says that during the phase of recollection in memory there is a sequence in the series of images and ideas that come back to one's (conscious) mind, since they had been previously stored in depth following an order of their own. Indeed, he proceeds to investigate the conditions under which these, seemingly haphazard, fragmented memories associate with each other (similarity, nearness, emotional condition, etc.). The paradigm given in *On Memory* of a chain of associations, milk-white-fog-humidity-autumn (see Chapter Six "Memory"), proves by itself what the philosopher wanted to impart.

Latent and manifest dream are concepts very useful in psychoanalytic therapy. The latent content consists of daytime's residues, thoughts, desires, and memories, as well as bodily impressions. This material, which exists in the unconscious, provides what is needed for the manifest dream to present itself. The task of the analysis is to uncover the images of the manifest dream and reveal the actual meanings of thoughts, emotions, and so on, resting in the latent content. Aristotle's syllogism about the processes of dreaming has the same train of ideas, showing the philosopher's ability to trace intrapsychic phenomena without any metaphysical, prophetic, or theocratic prejudices. His theory about the formation of dreams is also based on the daytime's residues, which are sensory impressions, thoughts, and ideas extruded from consciousness for various reasons and kept "in depth, in a latent condition" (his very words, 460b). During sleep and "when the obstacles are raised" (463b) the latent material displays itself as images in the manifest dream. The Stagirite adds the case of bodily or outside stimuli, like fever and noise (for more details see Chapter Seven "Consciousness—dreams"). He even mentions the incomprehensible "distorted dreams" (464b), again a concept with a term like in today's psychoanalytic vocabulary, and tries to explain them.

CHAPTER SEVENTEEN

Narcissism—self-love

Aristotle in two chapters (Book IX) of *Nicomachean Ethics,* as well as in *Eudemian Ethics,* and after discussing friendship from various aspects, ends up in a psychologically very important conclusion: Friendships are determined according to one's feelings for oneself. His position is explicit: If one does not love one's own self, one cannot offer any true friendship or love to somebody else.

Man has the right to self-love

The philosopher's argumentation proceeds as follows: A good (*agathos*) man, a man with a sound personality, chooses a friend and is ready to offer to him if they both have common principles and wishes, and if they prefer the same things. The friend should be consistent in his likes and dislikes, so that the good man can spend time with him in a pleasant atmosphere. The friend should also be in a position to share joys and sorrows with the good man.

The philosopher's second part of the arguments in his syllogism starts with a sort of title: "But the good man possesses the same feelings for himself" (1166a). And he explains: The good man with a mature personality has virtuous principles and values which he follows steadily. He is after good targets and acts accordingly for his own sake. He is not changeable in his likes and dislikes. He can have a pleasant behaviour towards a friend, but he is also satisfied if alone and feels pleasure whenever in company with himself. He can even suffer, as well as rejoice by himself, since he is a realist and sees things as they are, following permanent criteria.

The Stagirite investigates the bases of such a calm and self-sufficient disposition on behalf of the good man and mentions a few reasons: A mature personality respects life as the extreme good and considers Man's existence as beneficial. The good man is full of pleasant memories and hopes for the future. And most of all: "His mind is rich in ideas" (1166a), so he can be in a dialogue with himself. Furthermore, during this dialogue, it is very important that the good and prudent man "is in harmony with himself" (1166a)—that he has no conflicting opinions in his inner self.

Aristotle's view is explicitly phrased: such a wise man "is his own best friend and therefore should have the greatest love for himself" (1168b). We are presented with the personality of a man having a pleasant time with himself, satisfied with his life, full of confidence for his abilities, in harmony with and enjoying his thoughts, loving very much his own actions; in psychoanalytic terms one could say that such a man's libido takes as its object the subject's own self—therefore the philosopher is actually speaking about *Ego-libido.*

Freud (1921c) in his work *Group Psychology and the Analysis of the Ego* defines libido as "the energy of those instincts which have to do with all that may be comprised under the word love". Consequently, ego-libido is frequently called *Narcissistic-libido,* since it is love directed to oneself. Aristotle's description of the good and wise man's relationship to his own self is evidently one of self-love—and one is excused to speak in that case of *narcissism.* Indeed the philosopher for such a personality uses the adjective *phil-autos,* which means lover-of-self.

A brief parenthesis: The ancient philosopher examines the issue of self-love mainly from the moral aspect and believes that most people, however ordinary they may be, possess the good qualities that give them the right to self-love. In contrast, bad and wicked men cannot establish steady friendships because the relation with their selves is not even friendly. They are never satisfied, are uneasy all the time, have insatiable appetites, and their actions can be harmful to others and themselves.

The Stagirite raises another question—whether self-love is an egoistic trait of the personality or not. The issue may seem solely moral, but it ends up in a psychological conclusion. The philosopher first mentions the opinion of many people who criticize in a derogatory manner everyone who loves his own self and comments: "the realities of life disagree with such thoughts" (1168a). Then he differentiates: It all depends on the basic personality of a man. If he is bad and wicked, as has already been explained above, he is in an inner conflicting situation and cannot offer what is proper for a friend, but acts only for his own sake—which is really an egoistic behaviour. We have seen on the other hand that the good and prudent man (*agathos*) is self-sufficient enough so as to afford to act also for the sake of others. He is self-disciplined, logical, noble, and just, in his actions, restraining himself from passions. "All the friendly and loving feelings are derived from one's inner self", the philosopher concludes, and so for such a good man "it is necessary to be a self-lover, since he is thus (psychologically) able to benefit his fellow men" (1168b).

Interestingly enough, Freud (1916–17) has dealt with the subject of differentiation between egoism and narcissism. In *Introductory Lectures on Psycho-analysis*, he writes: "When we speak of egoism, we have in view only the individual's advantage; when we talk of narcissism we are also taking his libidinal satisfaction into account".

"A friend is another self"

According to psychoanalytic theory, the human child is characterized by its narcissistic libido, that is, for love and pleasure concerning its body and generally itself. With the psychobiological development of the human being, gradually part of his libido is directed to external objects and the *Object-libido* is present from then on in the course of his whole life. We have seen that Aristotle has a parallel idea when he says that the relationships with others originate from the relationships to oneself. "A man's friend is another self, since the feelings to the friend are an extension of those the man has for himself" (1166a) is a brief expression of this concept. In fact, his whole syllogism, which we discussed a little before, runs on the same line and is condensed in the phrase: "Friendships are determined according to one's feelings to oneself" (1166a).

In Freud's work *Beyond the Pleasure Principle* (1920g) it is clearly stated that both the ego-libido and the object-libido are of the same nature and only the direction of the libido differs. Something analogous is said by Aristotle in *Nicomachean Ethics* regarding the direction of love: "The extreme degree of love for a friend is similar to one's love for oneself" (1166b)—in both cases love of the same quality.

In *On Narcissism: An Introduction*, Freud (1914c) is of the opinion that when the object-libido is increased, the narcissistic-libido is decreased, and vice versa. In *Totem and Taboo* (1912–13) he adds that "the narcissistic organization is never wholly abandoned and the human being remains to some extent narcissistic even after he has found external objects for his libido". Aristotle does not deal with the issue of self-love quantitatively, but in *Eudemian Ethics* he writes: "love towards oneself is steadily present as long as one lives irrespective of difficulties" (1240b).

It is interesting that both Aristotle and Freud use the same example, that of the love of the mother for her children, to illustrate the change of direction of the libido from the ego to external objects. Freud (1914c), speaking of pregnant mothers, considers that the embryo is for them "like an extraneous body, to which, starting out from their narcissism, they can then give complete object-love". Aristotle says that "the person who acts for the sake of somebody else and out of what is good for him offers to the other, like a mother does for her children, is a true friend" (1166a).

Narcissistic object-choice is a psychoanalytic concept that states that in certain cases the establishment of a relationship to an object is based on the relationship of one to oneself. Aristotle's view on the subject is very similar, as one can gather from what we have discussed up to now and from some other clear statements of the philosopher. In *Nicomachean Ethics*, for instance, he says that "all loving feelings towards others are an extension of the loving feelings a person has for himself" (1168b). We have also mentioned at the beginning the Stagirite's opinion that "friendships are determined according to one's feelings for oneself". In *Eudemian Ethics* he writes: "From the characteristic attitudes of one to oneself one's ways and feelings to others are derived" (1240a).

The need for human relationships

Aristotle, in order to underline the need of everyone to develop human relationships, brings into discussion the question of whether a supremely happy man possessing all the goods needs friendships or not. His answer is positive giving three reasons: First, man is created by Nature so as to live with others, having all the natural potentialities to acquire the greatest of external goods, that is, friendships, which no one should deny him. Second, Man is also "a social and political being" (*zoon politikon*) (1169b) needing to pass time with his fellow-citizens, "not simply to eat and drink together like cattle, but in order to discuss and interchange thoughts and ideas" (1169b). In addition, there is a third reason for the generally considered happy man to have friends—an emotional one. For such a man, being among good friends, doing virtuous acts, is pleasant and sweet. Living alone and in isolation is hard for everyone, even the happy man, who, in the company of others, will be more active and will derive pleasure from his continuous expenditure of energy.

The deeply psychological way that Aristotle approaches the subject shows his opinion to be in agreement with the psychoanalytic theory that a mature person cannot remain in a narcissistic situation, but even when happy needs *object-relationships*.

The philosopher's observation acuity registers another interesting human phenomenon: The creator loves more whatever he himself creates. As paradigms, the Stagirite brings the case of craftsmen who love more the work of their own hands, and of poets who even to a greater degree are fond of their own poems, as an extension of themselves. The interpretation Aristotle gives for such an attitude is psychologically very interesting. Everybody loves his own existence, he says, but we exist by living in activity and "while acting a creator is, in a sense, his own work" (1168a). And to this identification of the creator with his work, the philosopher adds a significant remark: "The creator, therefore, loves his work, since he loves his own self" (1168a). So the creator loves the object as part of himself and as a consequence the love directed to the object is essentially belonging and coming back to the subject.

The whole dynamics expressed by Aristotle reminds one of the process of *secondary narcissism* described by Freud (1923b) in *The Ego and the Id*: "The libido which flows into the Ego owing to the identifications ... brings about its secondary narcissism ... this narcissism is one which has been drawn back from the objects".

CHAPTER EIGHTEEN

Pleasure (*hedone*)

Aristotle examines the subject of pleasure (*hedone*) from multiple aspects—its qualities, its role, its targets, and such like. To the moral question of whether pleasure is good or not, a question to which previous philosophers held various opinions, the Stagirite takes a realistic, human, down-to-earth position. He states that pleasure is a fact of everyday life, since "all those things which are acceptable by everybody we call existing-as-such" (1173a).

He adds several qualities: not all men receive a stimulus in the same way or at the same level of intensity—for some something is desirable and for others not so. There are special pleasures that are felt more by specialists; for instance, a nice melody is more pleasurable for a musician. The philosopher even registers a psychobiological phenomenon, that of the extinction rule. If one is under the effect of two stimuli at the same time, then the most delightful will expel the other; that is, a great joy will not allow us to pay attention to something else we are told at that moment. Pleasures increase an activity, is another observation of Aristotle; but, he continues, when they are appropriate to it and enjoyable by the performer. For instance, one who likes geometry is more efficient and accurate in solving geometrical problems because of the joy that he derives from doing so, while a musician would not.

In many works of the ancient philosopher, there are aspects of *hedone* with a parallel philosophical and psychological interest. One of these can be found in the *Nicomachean Ethics* (Books X 1–3 and II 3), where reading carefully even the first lines only, one will find many points of view on subjects which are still today being examined in psychological circles. I present here a free translation of some lines of Book X in which some fundamental elements of pleasure are recorded, intending to discuss them more analytically immediately below.

Probably it is now time for a discussion about pleasure, since pleasure seems to be deeply ingrained in our human race; that is why people educate the young using as a rudder pleasure and unpleasure (*hedone-lupe*) .... These extend for the whole of life having a directing influence and force towards virtue and happiness .... People choose the pleasant and run away from the painful. (1172a)

(I use the term "unpleasure" borrowing it from the psychoanalytic literature as opposite to pleasure [*hedone*], although *lupe* can be better translated as "displeasure" or "psychic pain".)

The two poles: pleasure–unpleasure

From the above passage, and from other Aristotelian texts, it becomes evident that *hedone–lupe* (pleasure–unpleasure, psychic pain) constitutes a main axis in the philosopher's way of thinking. With an objective, but close to the phenomena, eye, he makes the comment: "It is evident that people avoid unpleasure as something bad, while they prefer pleasure as something good—so these two are opposed to each other" (1173a). With this phrase, Aristotle establishes the two poles of an axis on which many of his discussions and arguments are based. In B3 of the *Nicomachean Ethics*, he says: "Every study, whether of virtue, politics or other, must deal with pleasure or psychic pain" (1105a).

There is a human approach to those two psychological conditions, an approach both emotional and of energetic activity. Pleasures and their opposites are feelings originating from things, people, and situations that one likes or dislikes, affecting one's behaviour, so that in the former case he pursues them, and in the latter, he runs away.

The above position of Aristotle can be directly paralleled to a corresponding basic theorization of psychoanalysis—that of pleasure–unpleasure (Lust–Unlust). In his book on instincts, Freud (1915c) writes: "The instinctual impulses are subjected to the influences of three great polarities that dominate mental life ... the pleasure/unpleasure is the economic polarity". (The other two are "activity/passivity" and "ego–external world".)

So the founder of psychoanalysis introduces another parameter in the subject, that of the instincts, which he accepts as the basis and the motivating force towards pleasure. In *The Interpretation of Dreams* (Freud, 1900a) he says: "Pleasure and unpleasure prove to be the only psychical quality attaching to the transpositions of instinctual energy". As an example, Freud brings the instinctual needs of Man for survival, since whenever Man is hungry the internal excitation increases, as well as the consequent disagreeable feelings, while if hunger is satisfied the tension decreases and pleasant sensory-and-psychic feelings follow.

Psychoanalysis accepts a biological process—that the neurons of the brain cannot withstand the excessive stimuli by the instincts and have to discharge them. Yet the quantitative parameter of the excitation is at the same time a psychic experience. The general rule established by Freud (although later he added some exceptions) is that an increased stimulation produces an unbearable feeling (unpleasure, Unlust), while its diminution is accompanied by a hedonistic feeling (pleasure, Lust).

In the same line of thought the pleasure principle was established, according to which "sensations of a pleasurable nature have not anything inherently impelling about them, whereas unpleasurable ones have it in the highest degree; the latter impel towards change" (Freud, 1923b). In the Aristotelian texts, recording of such a change is expressed on the behavioural level in the phrase: "People choose the pleasant and run away from the painful" (1172a).

The strength of pleasure and of instincts

Aristotle attributes to *hedone* and *lupe* decisive qualities like "a directing influence and force" (1172a), strong enough to affect

Man's character and life, since they are considered by the philosopher able to push towards virtue and happiness, or the opposite. Moreover, he states that something is more desirable when we prefer it not as a means for something else, but for its own sake—and people generally acknowledge that pleasure is for itself desirable. So the attraction that pleasure enforces is taken as almost omnipotent, since everybody chooses pleasure instead of anything else. In order to underline the strength of pleasure, the Stagirite refers to a saying by Heraclitus that it is more difficult to fight against pleasure than against one's own anger.

A similar attraction for pleasure is frequently found in the psychoanalytic literature. Directing Man towards pleasure is in the Freudian psychology a basic property of the instincts, which exert an insistent pressure to be quickly satisfied. A person experiences such a condition with excitement, is fully affected, and may have difficulty to control himself and not be carried away in view of the bait and the expectation of pleasure. According to Freud (1915c), the instincts show the high level of demands between the body and the mental apparatus.

The fact that behind the process towards pleasure a motivating force exists does not escape the attention of Aristotle. In his work *On the Soul* he presents a similar query and speaks of desires and appetites, which (as we have seen in Chapter Four "Volition [will] and psychomotor function") have the characteristics of what today's biology and psychology call "instincts". Desire, he says, is the appetite for "sweet" pleasure and, as a rule, it functions contrary to rational thinking: it demands an immediate satisfaction in an impulsive way.

Temporal development and pleasure

A characteristic of pleasure on which the views of both the ancient philosopher and the founder of psychoanalysis agree, is that Man since his birth and for his whole life has a tendency towards it—a tendency that at the beginning demands immediate satisfaction, but with the passing of years accepts a more realistic adaptation. Aristotle, we have seen, remarks that pleasure is "ingrained in the human race and for the whole of life". In *Nicomachean Ethics*, he adds: "It is difficult to erase this passion which has coloured all our years" (1105a). Nevertheless, he makes a temporal distinction: "Nobody would prefer to continue having the mentality of a child, simply in order to enjoy to a great extent the pleasures of childhood" (1174a). The philosopher, therefore, accepts that with the oncoming of maturity a person changes his ways of searching for pleasure in accordance with reality.

Freud (1920g) also accepts that the instincts urge for immediate satisfaction and pleasure since the first stages of the psychobiological development, that is, since infancy and childhood, and that with maturity attitudes change. The pleasure principle lasts throughout life, but year after year new ways for fulfillment are built and the reality principle prevails in many actions. The Ego of a mature person recognizes the environmental obstacles and tries to adapt by postponement of satisfaction and, as Freud (1920g) underlines in *Beyond the Pleasure Principle*, by "temporary toleration of unpleasure as a step on the long indirect road to pleasure".

Another parameter of pleasure is its change in time following a certain action and, on this, Aristotle and Freud have different opinions. The philosopher considers pleasure to be complete at any moment in time, in the sense that it constitutes a whole by itself and does not need any more time or additions to be felt as pleasure. Psychoanalysis, on the other hand, sees pleasure as changing in time, and more specifically that it is mounting gradually as long as the internal excitation is decreasing, while there is displeasure if the stimuli increase.

In addition to the above, the Stagirite, with his clear-sightedness and his caution to observe human behaviour before coming to conclusions, remarks that pleasure depends on the circumstances and the condition of a person at a certain period of time. He brings the following paradigm: Even in the case of something sweet, it will seem differently when somebody is healthy or when he is in fever. Also in bad or good disposition, pleasure will vary.

To the question of temporal relation of energy to pleasure, Aristotle's final opinion in one of his last writings in *Nicomachean Ethics* is that pleasure accompanies and supervenes a satisfactory action. "After any passion or activity either pleasure or psychic pain will follow" (1104b), he clearly states in Book II 3. So *hedone* is a consequence of an energy, which it finally completes, while at the same time it constitutes a desirable end. We saw that Freud for the same subject in *The Interpretation of Dreams* (1900a) writes that pleasure and unpleasure are psychic qualities "attached to the transpositions of energy", while pleasure is retained as the aim for final satisfaction.

It is probably not accidental, but rather due to the keen intellectual abilities of both, that Aristotle and Freud express themselves on a certain subject with similar words and phrases. Regarding the role of pleasure throughout life Aristotle characterizes pleasure a rudder according to which one steers his behaviour, while Freud calls pleasure a regulator of further processes.

A basic difference in their theorization (without their being altogether opposite) is the way Man has to follow in the long run, so as from the insistent demands of pleasure he will be able to reach a mature facing of reality. The Stagirite gives emphasis to the educational and moral aspects of the subject, and advises that the young through education will be gradually steered (having in mind the two poles *hedone–lupe*) to recognize the realities of life and know what will actually give pleasure and what psychic pain. The whole effort, therefore, which the philosopher declares, is a conscious one, both on behalf of the young man and his environment (see our discussion about *ethos* in Chapter Eleven "The responsibility of one's Self").

Freud spoke of the pleasure principle as an automatic regulator of the psychic processes, which basically constitutes an unconscious mechanism of the organism itself. Following a complicated process the Ego obtains such a maturity that it adopts the reality principle; of course, psychoanalysis does not deny that the environment also contributes to the building of a realistic handling of life's problems.

One should not omit to note that Aristotle's concept of *hedone* has a very great spectrum, in contrast to the narrower psychobiological view of Lust by psychoanalysis. It ranges from the simple sensory taste of sweetness and other somatic pleasures, for example, of smell or vision, to intellectual and emotional ones, like the enjoyment of music, of solving mathematical problems, of beautiful memories, or of high hopes. Indeed the philosopher considers that "these last experiences can in no way cause psychic pain, since they have no deficiencies" (1173b). It may interest scholars, as well as everyone who loves studying, that Aristotle adds gaining knowledge among the pleasures which involve no pains; moreover, his personal preference is shown in a comment in the concluding paragraph of Chapter Three, Book X: "It makes no difference whether pleasures necessarily follow these experiences, because we would choose them even if we would get no pleasure from them" (1174a).

REFERENCES

Aristotle

Eudemian Ethics

1214a	1240a & b
1221a & b	1241b
1235a & b	1242a & b
1237b	1244a & b
1239a	1245a

History of Animals

588a & b
608a & b
610a
612b
631b

Nicomachean Ethics

1102a & b	1116a	1164a
1103a & b	1119b	1166a & b
1104b	1134b	1168a & b

1105a
1106b
1109a & b

1111b
1112a & b
1113a
1114a & b
1143b
1149a
1152a
1155a & b
1156b
1159a
1161a & b
1162a
1169b
1171a

1172a
1173a & b
1174a

On Divination of Sleep

463a & b
464b

On Dreams

459a & b
460b
461a & b
462b

On Memory

449b
450a & b
451a & b
452a
453a

On Sleep

454 a & b
455b

On the Soul

403a & b
407b
408a & b
412a
414a & b
415a
416b
417a
425b
426a & b
427a & b
428a & b
429a

431b
432a & b
433a & b
434a

Physics

192b

Politics

1253a	1337a & b
1332a	1340a
1335a & b	1341b
1336a & b	1342a

Rhetoric

1369b
1378a
1389a & b
1390a & b

Bekker, I. (1831). *Aristotelis Opera*. Berlin: Reiner.

Freud, S. (1900a). *The Interpretation of Dreams. S.E., 5*. London: Hogarth.

Freud, S. (1912–13). *Totem and Taboo. S.E., 13*. London: Hogarth.

Freud, S. (1914c). *On Narcissism: An Introduction. S.E., 14*. London: Hogarth.

Freud, S. (1915c). *Instincts and their Vicissitudes. S.E., 14*. London: Hogarth.

Freud, S. (1916–17). *Introductory Lectures on Psycho-Analysis. S.E., 16*. London: Hogarth.

Freud, S. (1920g). *Beyond the Pleasure Principle. S.E., 18*. London: Hogarth.

Freud, S. (1921c). *Group Psychology and the Analysis of the Ego. S.E., 18*. London: Hogarth.

Freud, S. (1923b). *The Ego and the Id. S.E., 19*. London: Hogarth.

Laplanche, J. & Pontalis, J. -B. (1985). *The Language of Psycho-analysis*. London: Hogarth.

INDEX

For Product Safety Concerns and Information please contact our EU representative GPSR@taylorandfrancis.com Taylor & Francis Verlag GmbH, Kaufingerstraße 24, 80331 München, Germany

Batch number: 10726011

Printed by Printforce, the Netherlands